To   Lewis, Steven and Duke

CONTENTS

INTRODUCTION

This book deals with the basic principles of statistical methods. The goal is to introduce the ideas and concepts which are fundamental to the understanding of modern statistics. Statistical data and statistical techniques play essential roles in many decision-making and forecasting situations and it is becoming more apparent that anyone requiring to understand the implications of much numerical work needs at least an acquaintance with the subject of statistics.

It is assumed that the reader has a fairly limited mathematical background and some mathematical detail is omitted. It is important that the meaning and implications of basic concepts are understood, but it is hoped to avoid the reader getting lost in an excessive amount of detail which may cloud the important issues.

Within the subject area of statistics learning by example is the most appropriate way of attaining a grasp of the subject.

Statistical techniques are best understood by using them rather than by committing them to memory. In this book, the examples used fall into two categories; simple ones used to illustrate a single point or introduce a new method, and more difficult ones comparable with those set in examinations.

A particularly important feature of the book is the inclusion of a number of exercises at the end of each chapter to cover the subject matter. Answers are provided to these questions.

_____ **1** _____

DATA AND ITS PRESENTATION

1.1   INTRODUCTION

One of the fundamental aims of statistics is to make sense of a mass of unorganised data. To fully appreciate the information presented by a mass of figures some order or system must be brought about.

In this chapter we look at some of the ways of presenting data. Basically this involves making data more informative, more interesting, more acceptable and also in many cases more manipulative for mathematical purposes.

When collecting information, we want to find out about a particular characteristic of a set of people or objects e.g. the values of properties, the weights of materials etc.

The particular characteristic in which we are interested, is called the **variable** because it varies from one member of a group to another.

1.2   ORGANISING DATA: FREQUENCY TABLES

The following figures show the thickness, to the nearest mm, of twenty five concrete blocks which a manufacturer has selected from his stock.

98	99	99	102	100
101	102	99	100	99
100	102	101	100	101
103	100	98	98	100
97	100	102	100	103

Data presented in this manner, as a collection of single facts, are not very meaningful. To make these figures useful it is necessary to organise them in some systematic manner.

A good method of doing this is to draw up a **frequency (distribution) table**, which is so called because it shows the frequency with which the various figures occur.

The way to tabulate these data is to write down, in order, the different thicknesses and count how many times each figure occurs. This counting can be facilitated by the use of tally marks; a stroke being placed against a figure each time it occurs and every fifth stroke being drawn diagonally across the previous four to make groups of five. The number of times each value occurs is called the frequency (designated by the letter 'f') of that value.

Table 1.1 shows the tabulation results.

Table 1.1: Frequency distribution of thickness of concrete blocks

mm	*Tally*	*Frequency (f)*
97	1	1
98	111	3
99	1111	4
100	1111 111	8
101	111	3
102	1111	4
103	11	2
		25

This simple organisation of the figures often provides a first step towards obtaining statistical information.

1.3   GROUPING OF DATA

Sometimes the data we are considering contain a large range of values and it is necessary to collect the data into groups.

The following are the rating valuation assessments (in £s) of forty retail properties in a certain area.

158	176	188	208	183
190	216	184	184	191
164	174	154	186	178
186	202	179	185	183
177	198	182	174	193
164	197	170	179	162
167	178	173	182	194
192	199	194	177	169

These figures are widely spread out (the lowest value being 154 and the highest 216) and to draw up a frequency table similar to the one in the previous example would produce an unwieldy and impractical table.

In such a case as this, it is customary to group or classify the data. The figures are grouped into what are called **class intervals** and a frequency for each group is obtained.

The main problem lies in choosing the class intervals to use. This choice is basically a matter of judgement. It really depends upon what we want to do with the data once they have been classified. The class intervals should not be so large as to lose much of the information obtained from the original data e.g. if the rating valuations were merely categorised into those below £190 and those £190 and above, much of the relevance of the valuations would be lost. On the other hand, classification into groups with a range of, say, just two or three marks would defeat the purpose of grouping.

In this example, as a happy medium, the marks have been classified as shown in Table 1.2.

Table 1.2:   Frequency distribution of rating valuations

£	Tally	Frequency (f)
150 - 159	11	2
160 - 169	⊔⊔1	5
170 - 179	⊔⊔1 ⊔⊔1 1	11
180 - 189	⊔⊔1 ⊔⊔1	10
190 - 199	⊔⊔1 1111	9
200 - 209	11	2
210 - 219	1	1
		40

This classification enables us to obtain an immediate picture of the distribution of the valuations i.e. a clustering of valuations in the £170s, £180s and £190s and fewer properties with valuations at either extreme. Therefore, one objective of neatly displaying the information contained in the raw data has already been achieved.

However, one point to be noted, which will be important at a later stage, is that some accuracy must, by necessity, be lost when the figures are grouped e.g. from Table 1.2 we can see that five properties had valuations between £160 and £169 but we cannot tell that they were £162, £164, £167 and £169 respectively.

Choice of class boundaries. Several factors were taken into consideration in this example.

1. Each class had to be mutually exclusive with no gaps to be left between classes. This meant that any valuation could be assigned to just one class. It would have been impossible to have classes £150 - £160, £160 - £170 etc. Into which class could we place a valuation of £160?

2. Class intervals were chosen that were easy to read and use e.g. intervals of 5, 10 or 100 units are mentally easier to cope with.

3. Equal class intervals were chosen. Generally speaking a frequency table is 'easier' to read if the classes are of equal length. In this example, our data are likely to be of most use when categorised as valuations in the £150s, in the £160s etc.
    However, this is certainly not a hard and fast rule, and circumstances often dictate that frequency tables contain classes of varying length especially at the beginning or end of tables.

4. The first class began with £150. There would have been little point in having classes £130-£139, £140-£149, for instance, as this would not have added any extra information to the table. The lowest and highest values in the data (i.e. £154 and £216) were important in deciding on the first and last classes for the table.

It is worthwhile at this point to distinguish between **discrete and continuous variables.**

A variable is discrete if it can only have a finite number of values, or usually as many values as there are whole numbers. The number of people living in an area, for example, is a discrete variable because it has to be a whole number.

In contrast, a continuous variable is one which can assume any value along a continuous scale. Length, weight and time are all continuous variables, even though in practice the way in which these variables are measured and rounded off (e.g. to the nearest mm, kg or second) makes them discrete.

If the class intervals in our example were plotted on a scale, there would be gaps between the classes.

This did not really matter in this case because all the valuations were given in whole pounds. If the values had been put to the nearest penny the class limits, ie the smallest and largest values which could fall in a particular class, would have had to have been changed from, for example, £150 - 159 to £150.00 - £159.99 to accommodate all the possible values.

In certain circumstances, we may wish to eliminate the gaps altogether and in that case we may have to define class limits. For the first class the lower class limit would be £149.51 and the upper class limit £159.50; for the second class the lower class limit would be £159.51 and the upper class limit £169.50, etc.

Open-ended classes. When dealing with data in which just one or a few values are much greater (or smaller) than the rest of the values then an open-ended class can be used in the frequency table.

If there had been just one property in our example with a rating valuation of say £283, the simplest way of incorporating this into the table would have been to add one extra class to the existing table by putting:

£	f
.	.
.	.
220 and above	1

Similarly, a single relatively low valuation of, say, £108 would have meant an extra initial class such as:

£	f
Under 150	1
.	.
.	.
.	.

The extra class in both these cases is termed an open-ended class and has only one class limit.

1.4   CUMULATIVE FREQUENCY

It is often useful to arrange the data from a frequency distribution into a **cumulative frequency distribution**.

In many situations we may wish to know how many values fall above or below certain limits rather than how many fall in a particular class.

Table 1.3 shows a frequency distribution of the marks (out of 100) of 50 students in a surveying examination.

The students may obtain different levels of grading according to whether they obtained certain marks and so we could accumulate the frequencies in two different ways.

Firstly, to construct a cumulative *'less than'* distribution, from the first class in Table 1.3 we can see that only 1 student obtained less than 10 marks. Looking at the second class as well, by adding the frequency for the second class to the frequency for the first class, we find that $(2 + 1) = 3$ students obtained less than 20 marks.

Table 1.3:   Frequency distribution of marks in a surveying examination

Mark	f
0 - 9	1
10 - 19	2
20 - 29	4
30 - 39	4
40 - 49	7
50 - 59	15
60 - 69	9
70 - 79	3
80 - 89	2
90 - 99	3
	50

The cumulative distribution resulting from this procedure is shown in Table 1.4. Note that the last value in the cumulative frequency column must be the same as the total frequency.

Table 1.4 gives us information on how many students failed to achieve certain marks. It may be of greater interest to cumulate the frequencies beginning at the other end

6

and draw up an *'or more'* distribution as in Table 1.5.

There are 3 students with 90 or more marks, as can be seen from the last class in Table 1.5, and if we add the frequency for the penultimate class to this, we find that there are (3 + 2) = 5 students who obtained 80 or more marks. This adding procedure, going back one class each time, gives us the full table.

Table 1.4: Cumulative *'less than'* distribution of surveying examination results

Mark	Cumulative Frequency
Less than 10	1
Less than 20	3
Less than 30	7
Less than 40	11
Less than 50	18
Less than 60	33
Less than 70	42
Less than 80	45
Less than 90	47
Less than 100	50

Table 1.5: Cumulative *'or more'* distribution of examination marks

Mark	Cumulative Frequency
0 or more	50
10 or more	49
20 or more	47
30 or more	43
40 or more	39
50 or more	32
60 or more	17
70 or more	8
80 or more	5
90 or more	3

We could also have drawn up a cumulative *'or less'* table i.e. '9 or less', '19 or less' etc, but this would give the same cumulative frequencies as in Table 1.4 and as the pass marks for the examination gradings are usually set at the 10 mark points the table shown is preferred.

Similarly Table 1.5 is preferred to a cumulative *'more than'* table i.e. 'more than 89' etc. in the particular example.

1.5 GRAPHICAL PRESENTATIONS OF DATA

Having put data into a frequency table, one common follow-up is to present the data in a graphical form in order that essential features of the frequency distribution can be displayed.

1.5.1 Histograms

One way of representing a frequency distribution graphically is by means of a histogram. On the graph, the values or measurements are represented on the horizontal scale, and the frequencies on the vertical scale.

Rectangular blocks are then drawn, the bases of which are determined by the values - or class intervals in the case of grouped data - in the frequency table. The heights of the blocks are determined by the corresponding frequencies.

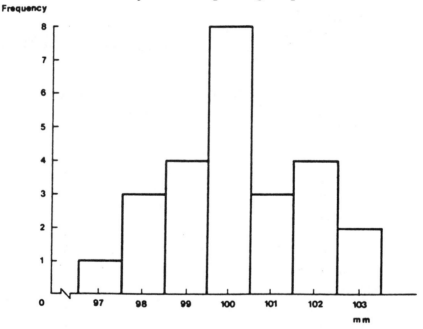

Fig 1.1:   Histogram from Table 1.1

Figure 1.1 shows a histogram plotted from the information contained in Table 1.1. The centre of each block is set against the value which it represents on the horizontal axis.

In the case of grouped data, on the horizontal scale we can either indicate the class

8

boundaries or, more usually, if we want to make the histogram easier to understand, we can use more approximate key values.

Figure 1.2 shows a histogram plotted from the grouped data in Table 1.2. The width of each block is 10 units on the horizontal scale. To be strictly accurate we should take the class boundaries such as £159.5 and £169.5 as the boundaries of each block, but the presentation is improved here if the values of £160, £170 etc. are used instead.

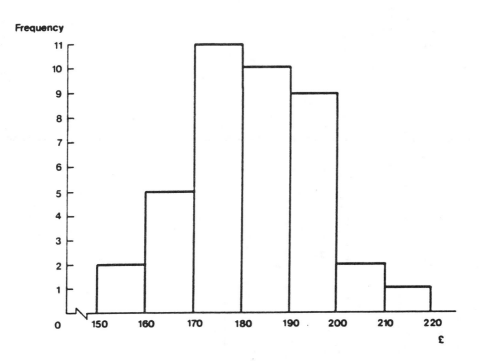

Fig 1.2: Histogram from Table 1.2

The rule that class intervals should be equal is often broken. Care has to be taken that a histogram is not misleading, as it indeed might be if adjustments are not made in the case of a distribution with unequal class intervals.

Table 1.6 shows the data on rating valuation assessments when all valuations from £160 to £179 are put into one class.

The histogram which corresponds to the frequency distribution is shown in Figure 1.3.

This histogram misrepresents the data in the sense that it probably gives the impression that the majority of the valuations lie in the £160 to £180 range, whereas this is not actually the case.

Table 1.6:   Altered frequency distribution of rating valuations

£	Frequency (f)
150 - 159	2
160 - 179	16
180 - 189	10
190 - 199	9
200 - 209	2
210 - 219	1
	40

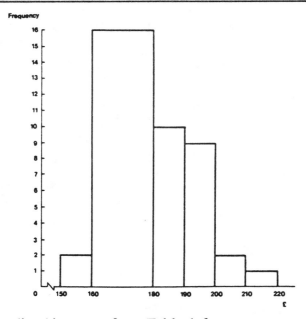

Fig 1.3:   Misleading histogram from Table 1.6

To rectify this misleading picture, we need to adjust the histogram block representing the second class. This involves dividing the frequency of the class by two and then drawing the block to this new height of 8.

10

Generally, if one class is twice as large as the others we divide its frequency by two; if three times as large, divide by three etc.

The assumption implicit in this adjustment is that a half of the 16 values in this class fall in the £160-£169 group and the other 8 fall in the £170-£179 group.

The adjusted histogram is shown in Fig 1.4.

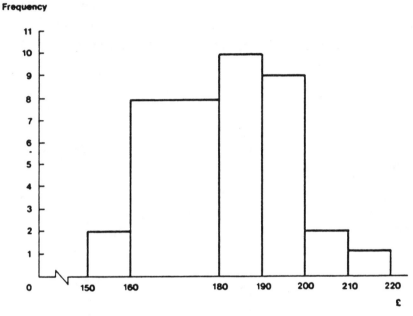

Fig 1.4:   Adjusted histogram from Table 1.6

It is the area of each block which represents the relative importance of each class and not just the height of the block.

Finally, it needs to be mentioned that a histogram is not really suitable for dealing with open-ended classes. If it is essential, however, that an attempt be made to draw such a diagram, the block for the open-ended class is best displayed as being of the same width as the adjacent block and the class limit of the end block labelled 'or more' or 'less than' etc. according to the particular requirement.

1.5.2 Frequency polygons

Another common form of graphic representation of a frequency table is the **frequency polygon**.

It can be drawn quite simply by plotting the frequency associated with each value - or the mid-point of the class interval in the case of grouped data - and then connecting these points by straight lines.

If a histogram has already been drawn, the mid-points of the tops of the blocks can be joined together with straight lines to form the polygon. However, it is not necessary to construct a histogram before drawing the polygon, and given a choice between the two types of diagram to represent certain distributions, it is common practice to use a histogram for discrete distributions and a frequency polygon for data where continuity is likely.

A frequency polygon representing the data on rating valuations is shown in Fig.1.5. In order to neaten the diagram, the polygon here is drawn down to points on the horizontal axis by adding an extra class to either end and these classes obviously have frequencies of zero.

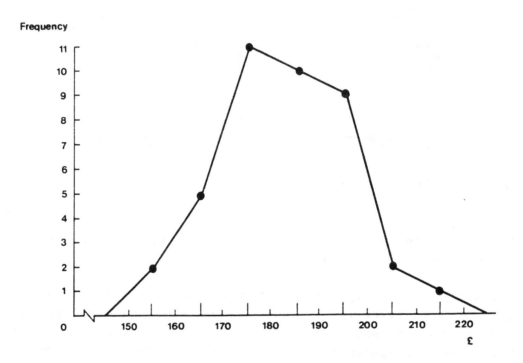

Fig 1.5: Frequency polygon from Table 1.2

1.5.3 Frequency curves

The idea of representing frequencies by areas, which forms the basis of a histogram, can also be utilised if continuous curves are used to join the plotted frequency points. Obviously the greater the number of classes represented by a histogram, the more closely the block diagram can approximate to a curve, but even with our data on rating valuations this idea can be shown.

Figure 1.6 shows a frequency curve superimposed on the histogram for these data. We are able to say from this diagram that, for instance, the number of valuations less than £160 is approximately represented by the shaded area under the curve.
The importance of this use of frequency curves will become apparent in further statistical work in ensuing chapters.

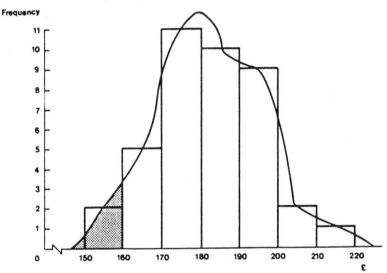

Fig 1.6:   Frequency curve and histogram from Table 1.2

1.5.4 Ogives

So far we have been concerned with drawing diagrams to represent frequency distributions. By applying the method of constructing a frequency polygon to a cumulative distribution we can draw a polygon called an ogive - so called from a term used in architecture for the characteristic shape formed by this cumulative frequency polygon.

Figure 1.7 shown ogives used to depict the cumulative frequency distributions in Tables 1.4 and 1.5. Here the cumulative frequencies are plotted instead of the ordinary frequencies.

Unlike the frequency polygon, though, the points are not plotted against the class mark, i.e. the middle of the class interval. In the 'less than' ogive, the cumulative frequencies are plotted against the upper class boundaries of 9.5, 19.5 etc. This is to differentiate this ogive from an 'or less' ogive.

There is obviously a difference between 'less than 10' and '10 or less' and we need to show this.

In the 'or more' ogive, however, the cumulative frequencies can be plotted against the 10, 20, 30 etc. marks.

The ogive is often used for calculation problems, as we shall see in the next chapter, and so we usually join the points together by straight lines and not curves on the assumption that the items in each group are evenly spread between the boundaries of each class interval.

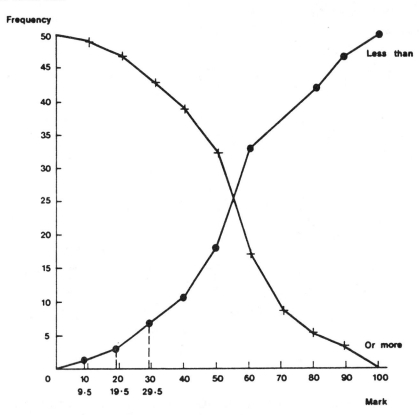

Fig 1.7: Cumulative frequency curves (ogives) from Tables 1.4 and 1.5

1.6 OTHER METHODS OF DISPLAYING DATA

So far we have only been concerned with diagrams which are used to display data from frequency tables. There are many other methods of pictorial display of data and some of these are considered below.

1.6.1 Bar charts

A bar chart consists of bars of different heights drawn to depict the total number of items in a group. The blocks are always of equal width and usually differ from histogram blocks in that they do not normally have a scale measured along their base axis. (Note: A horizontal bar chart may sometimes be used instead of a vertical one).

Example 1.1:

Table 1.7 shows the numbers of houses of various types sold by two estate agents in a particular month.

A bar chart displaying the data in this table is shown in Figure 1.8. Note that to make for easy understanding of the diagram, shading of the bars and a key have been used and also the same order of the different categories has been used.

To make it easier to compare the overall total sales of the two estate agents, while still being able to see the breakdown into the different categories of property, component bar charts may be used instead, as in Figure 1.9.

Another variation of the bar chart to consider is the percentage component bar chart.

This is mainly used when it is important to view the relative importance of the various components.

Table 1.7: Number of residential properties sold

Estate Agent	A	B
Town Houses	8	6
Semi-Detached	12	8
Detached	5	6
	25	20

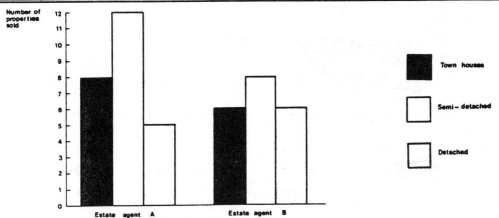

Fig 1.8: Bar charts from Table 1.7

Fig 1.9: Component bar charts

In Figure 1.10, the two sets of figures for comparison are portrayed by bars of equal length and the bars are split into their various components on the basis of the relative importance in percentage terms.

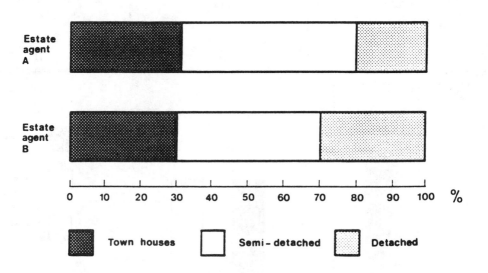

Fig 1.10: Percentage bar charts

16

The percentage values are shown in Table 1.8.

Table 1.8: Percentage value of houses sold

	Estate Agent A	Estate Agent B
Town Houses	8/25 x 100 = 32%	6/20 x 100 = 30%
Semi-Detached	12/25 x 100 = 48%	8/20 x 100 = 40%
Detached	5/25 x 100 = 20%	6/20 x 100 = 30%

1.6.2 Pie charts

These diagrams are commonly used to represent data where ratios or relative values are important.

A pie chart is a circle divided into segments, the sizes of which are proportionate to the sizes of the components they represent.

To construct a pie chart, the percentage of the total, attributable to each component needs to be found and each percentage then multiplied by 360/100 to obtain the number of degrees to assign to each component.

We have already calculated the percentage of sales made up by each category of property for estate agent A in Table 1.8. Multiplying each percentage by 360/100, we obtain the following:

Town houses $\quad$ 32% x 360/100 = 115.2°

Semi-detached $\quad$ 48% x 360/100 = 172.8°

Detached $\quad$ 20% x 360/100 = 72°

The pie chart of this data is shown is Figure 1.11. Pie charts have a major advantage in that they show how one whole set of data is divided into various components and it is easy to see what size these components are in relation to each other and to the whole set.

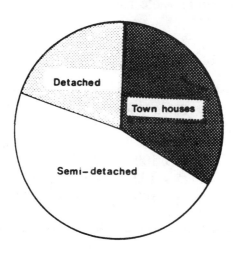

Fig 1.11: Pie chart

1.6.3 Pictograms

Finally, one of the most common and striking ways of illustrating statistics is by means of a graph employing forms of pictures.

Small pictures of a particular object to portray the object involved are used, e.g. houses for construction data, coins for expenditure, people for employment etc.

Examples of this type of diagram are in frequent use in the media, so just one case is presented here.

Table 1.9 shows the number of houses sold by a group of estate agencies over a three year period.

Table 1.9: House sales 1992-94

Year	Sales
1992	456
1993	272
1994	579

A pictogram, whereby one small house represents 100 from the table, is shown in Figure 1.12.

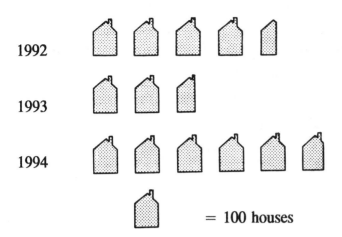

Fig 1.12: Pictogram

Pictograms certainly have an advantage over the other types of diagram when it comes to attracting attention to the main features of the data portrayed, but cannot really play a part in any detailed statistical work because of their lack of precision.

Only a few of the more common types of diagram have been considered in this section. There are many different variations of the bar charts, pie diagrams and pictograms and really a great deal of flexibility is permissible in the drawing up of these diagrams. The main concern is that a diagram conveys its information in a concise and interesting manner.

Many examples of these various diagrams can be seen in trade journals, newspapers, etc. and it should be an interesting exercise to the reader to look at these diagrams in practice.

1.7   EXERCISES

1.   The following marks were obtained by 50 building students in an examination.

94	40	70	57	48
56	75	67	62	67
25	53	52	43	55
45	49	55	45	53
58	44	74	63	42
50	65	59	46	36
59	25	77	54	23
33	83	47	43	52
29	47	61	50	37
79	41	51	63	49

(a)   tabulate the results in the form of a frequency distribution;

(b)   plot the result of (a) in the form of a histogram;

(c)   construct a cumulative frequency table and plot the ogive from this table.

2.   It is said that 'one picture is worth a thousand words.' How far might it also be correctly said that a picture is worth a thousand numbers? Discuss this in relation to the use of pictorial and other diagrammatic methods, in presenting various types of statistical data for various purposes to differing sorts of reader.

_____ **2** _____

MEASURES OF LOCATION

2.1   INTRODUCTION

So far, two basic methods of dealing with sets of figures have been considered. Statistics have been put into tabulated form and into diagrammatic form. This type of exercise on its own, though, does not tell us very much about the characteristics of a group of numbers.

2.2   MEASURES OF CENTRAL TENDENCY

A measure of central tendency (or average) represents an attempt to produce one value from a whole set of data which can be regarded as representative of all the items.
There are several types of average employed in statistical analysis, but we shall concentrate on three of the more important ones.

-        The arithmetic mean
-        The median
-        The mode

2.3   THE ARITHMETIC MEAN

This is what the layman would normally calculate if asked to find the average of a group of numbers, and is hereinafter referred to as just the mean. It is found by dividing the sum of the values by the number of items (or total frequency).

Example 2.1:

The numbers of properties sold by an estate agency over an eleven-week period were:

$$6 \quad 8 \quad 8 \quad 4 \quad 3 \quad 10 \quad 8 \quad 1 \quad 4 \quad 1 \quad 2$$

$$\text{The mean} = \frac{\text{Sum of values}}{\text{Number of weeks}} = \frac{55}{11} = 5 \text{ properties}$$

2.3.1 *Finding the mean from a frequency table*

Ungrouped data:

We can return to the example in the previous chapter (section 1.2) where the data on concrete building blocks were put into a frequency table.

It is possible to find the mean from the tabulated data by simply multiplying each value (mm) in the table by the corresponding frequency, summing the results and dividing the total by the total number of blocks.

It is worthwhile at this point introducing a symbolic notation into the calculations we are making.

As previously we can denote the frequency by the letter f, and we shall denote the column of values in the table by the letter x.   Each value multiplied by its corresponding frequency is therefore fx.

When adding together all these fx products we write the total sum as Σfx, as the Greek letter Σ is a short-hand way of writing 'the sum of'.   The total number of values we can therefore write as Σf i.e. the sum of the frequencies.

So our formula for the mean of tabulated data can be written:

$$\overline{x} = \frac{\Sigma fx}{\Sigma f}$$

where $\overline{x}$ (pronounced x-bar) signifies the mean of the x's.

Table 2.1 shows the tabulated data on brick thicknesses.

$$\overline{x} = \frac{\Sigma fx}{\Sigma f} = \frac{2504}{25} = 100.1 mm$$

Table 2.1: Frequency distribution of brick thicknesses

Brick Thickness (mm): x	f	fx
97	1	97
98	3	294
99	4	396
100	8	800
101	3	303
102	4	408
103	2	206
	Σf = 25	Σfx = 2 504

Grouped data:

When using a similar procedure to find the mean of the grouped data, a specific assumption is made concerning the values which fall in any particular class.

If we take as an example just one class from the frequency table of surveying examination marks in Table 1.3:

Marks   f
20-29   4

We do not know without referring back to the original raw data what the exact marks of these four surveying students were - this loss of information being inevitable in the classification process. What we do, therefore, is to relate the frequency to the midpoint or class mark of each class. The midpoint of a class is found by adding together the first and last possible values in a class and dividing by two. So here the midpoint is:

$$\frac{20 + 29}{2} = 24.5$$

When finding the mean, what we are basically assuming is that this value of 24.5 represents the whole class 20-29.

24.5 and the other midpoints from the frequency table are used as the x values to which the frequencies are applied.

23

We can now use Table 2.2, which shows the classified surveying marks to find the mean.

$$\overline{x} = \frac{\Sigma fx}{\Sigma f} = \frac{2655}{50} = 53.1 \; marks$$

Table 2.2: Classified surveying marks

Marks	Midpoint		
	x	f	fx
0 - 9	4.5	1	4.5
10 - 19	14.5	2	29.0
20 - 29	24.5	4	98.0
30 - 39	34.5	4	138.0
40 - 49	44.5	7	311.5
50 - 59	54.5	15	817.5
60 - 69	64.5	9	580.5
70 - 79	74.5	3	223.5
80 - 89	84.5	2	169.0
90 - 99	94.5	3	283.5
		Σf = 50	Σfx = 2 655.0

2.3.2 The assumed-mean method

The calculation involved in finding the mean from classified data can often be simplified by working from an assumed mean, which is then adjusted appropriately.

If we take the classified data on rating valuations from the previous chapter (as shown in Table 1.2) we could find the mean by firstly guessing at what the mean will be by inspection. We will take £184.5 as our estimate. (Note that this value is a midpoint of one of the classes; it simplifies matters if a midpoint value is chosen as the assumed mean.)

The procedure is then to find by how much the other midpoints deviate from the assumed mean, to multiply each deviation (d) by the appropriate frequency and to sum these df products.

The mean of the deviations ($=\Sigma df/\Sigma f$) is then used to adjust the assumed mean to the

24

true mean. This procedure is illustrated in Table 2.3.

Table 2.3: Procedure to find mean by the assumed mean method

Rating Valuation (£)	Midpoint	Deviation From Assumed Mean of 184.5 (d)	f	df
150 - 159	154.5	-30	2	-60
160 - 169	164.5	-20	5	-100
170 - 179	174.5	-10	11	-110
180 - 189	184.5	0	10	0
190 - 199	194.5	10	9	90
200 - 209	204.5	20	2	40
210 - 219	214.5	30	1	30
			$\Sigma f = 40$	$\Sigma df = -110$

The mean of the deviations $= \dfrac{\Sigma df}{\Sigma f} = \dfrac{-110}{40} = -2.75$

The true mean = assumed mean + the mean of the deviations
= 184.5 + (-2.75)
= £181.75

2.3.3 Weighted means

In some situations it is unsatisfactory to calculate the mean of a set of items without taking account of the relative importance of certain items. In such circumstances it is appropriate to calculate a weighted mean.

The following example shows the use of a weighted mean. A builder's merchant sells three types of screen wall blocks (types A, B and C) and he makes 10 pence, 20 pence and 30 pence profit respectively on each unit that he sells. His records show that for every 5 blocks of type A that he sells, he is able to sell 3 blocks of type B and 2 blocks of type C.

If we want to find the merchant's mean profit per unit sold, we should not merely add together 10, 20 and 30 and divide by 3 to give a mean of 20 pence. Instead, the three profit figures should be weighted according to how important each type of block is in the merchant's sales.

We find a weighted mean by attaching weights to each of the profit figures and then dividing by the total weights. The general formula is:

$$Weighted\ mean(\overline{X}_W) = \frac{W_1X_1 + W_2X_2 + \ldots + W_nX_n}{W_1 + W_2 + \ldots + W_n}$$

where

$x_1, x_2, \ldots x_n$ = the n items for which we wish to find the mean

$w_1, w_2, \ldots w_n$ = the weights attached to each item $x_1, x_2, \ldots x_n$ respectively.

So in our example the x's are the profit figures and the w's are taken from the sales figures. We have then:

$x_1 = 10$ $\quad$ $x_2 = 20$ $\quad$ $x_3 = 30$
$w_1 = 5$ $\quad$ $w_2 = 3$ $\quad$ $w_3 = 2$

Putting these figures into the formula gives:

$$\overline{X}_w = \frac{10(5) + 20(3) + 30(2)}{5 + 3 + 2}$$

$$= \frac{170}{10} = 17\ pence$$

As we shall see in a later chapter, this type of 'averaging' using weights is often a necessary procedure in the composition of index numbers.

2.4 THE MEDIAN

When a number of values are arranged in numerical (ascending or descending) order, the median is the middle value.

If the figures on property sales from Example 2.1 are put into ascending order, we have:

1 $\quad$ 1 $\quad$ 2 $\quad$ 3 $\quad$ 4 $\quad$ 4 $\quad$ 6 $\quad$ 8 $\quad$ 8 $\quad$ 8 $\quad$ 10

The middle value is the 6th one and is 4. The simple rule is to take the value of the ((n + 1)/2)th item in a series, where n is the total number of items. So in this example, because we have an odd number of values, we had an exact item in the list to refer to.

If we had only ten figures in our original list e.g. if the last figure, 2, had been omitted, the ordered figures would have been:

| 1 | 1 | 3 | 4 | 4 | 6 | 8 | 8 | 8 | 10 |

and the median value is the ((10 + 1)/2)th in the list which means it is midway between the 5th and 6th values. The median is, therefore, (4 + 6)/2 = 5

2.4.1 Finding the median from a frequency table

Ungrouped data:

Once data have been put into frequency table form, they have already been put into numerical order so it is a relatively easy matter to read off the appropriate value from the table.

In the frequency table on brick thickness (Table 2.1) the total frequency is 25 and so the median value is that of the ((25 + 1)/2)th = 13th. To find out what this value is we can refer to the appropriate cumulative frequency table (Table 2.4). From the table it can be seen that there are 8 bricks with thicknesses of 99mm or less, and 16 with thicknesses of 100mm or less.

The middle one (the 13th) must therefore be one of those with a thickness of 100mm.

Table 2.4: Cumulative frequency table for brick thicknesses

Brick Thickness (mm)	Cumulative Frequency
97 or less	1
98 or less	4
99 or less	8
100 or less	16 <———
101 or less	19
102 or less	23
103 or less	25

Grouped data:

From classified frequency tables we can find the class containing the median value in a manner similar to that just described, but then have the additional problem of locating the median within the appropriate class. The data on rating valuations are illustrated in Table 2.5.

The median of a set of grouped data is worked out according to a slightly different formula than for ungrouped data. The median is the value of the $n/2$th item. So here we are interested in the rating valuation of the 20th property.

Table 2.5: Rating valuations

Rating Valuation Assessment (£)	Number of Properties	Cumulative Frequency
Less than 160	2	2
160 but less than 170	5	7
170 but less than 180	11	18
180 but less than 190	10	28
190 but less than 200	9	37
200 but less than 210	2	39
210 but less than 220	1	40

It can be seen from the table that this property has a rating valuation somewhere between £180 and £189. We now make an assumption that the valuations of the 10 properties in this class are evenly distributed between the two class limits. The 20th property overall is the 2nd out of the 10 in this class and so we assume that this valuation is 2/10th of the way along this class interval.

The class interval here is from the lower class boundary of £179.5 to the upper class boundary of £189.5 and is therefore equivalent to £10.

The 20th property is assumed to be located at a point 2/10 of the way along this interval of 10 which begins at £179.5 i.e.

$$\text{the median valuation} = 179.5 + (^2/_{10} \times 10)$$
$$= £181.5$$

This general formula for finding the median for grouped data can be presented more formally as:

$$Median = L_m + \left[\frac{\frac{n}{2} - F_{m-1}}{f_m} \right] \times C$$

where

L_m =   the lower class boundary of the median group.
C   =   the class interval.
F_{m-1} =   the cumulative frequency for the preceding group.
f_m =   the frequency of the median group.

2.4.2 Finding the median from an ogive

The median can be found graphically quite simply from an ogive.

From the plotted curve, the value of the middle item from the cumulative frequency scale is read off.

Figure 2.1 shows the 'less than' ogive for the rating valuation data in Table 2.5. We can read off from the ogive the value corresponding to the 20th property as £181.5.

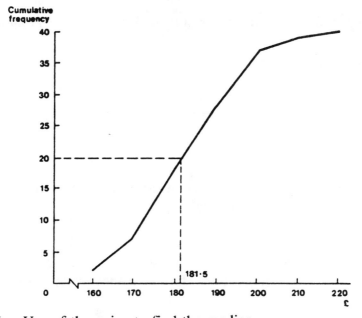

Fig 2.1:   Use of the ogive to find the median

29

2.5   THE MODE

The mode may be defined as the value which occurs most often.

Whenever we have unclassified data, there is no calculation required at all for the mode. It is found merely by the selection of the value with the highest frequency.

From the data in Example 2.1, the value which occurs most commonly is 8. On three occasions this number of properties were sold and no other value occurs three times.

To find the mode from a frequency table such as Table 2.1 is a simple matter. The value 100mm has a frequency of 8 and is the most common value.

With a classified frequency table it is easy to select the modal class and often that is all that we are concerned with. Difficulties arise, though, when we wish to decide exactly where within the modal group, the mode lies.

We could assume that the items in the class are evenly distributed and choose the midpoint as our estimate, but if we look at the frequency table on rating valuations in Table 2.3, the justification for doing this might be questioned. The modal class is 170 to 179 but there are twice as many valuations between 180 and 189 as between 160 and 169.

It is therefore quite valid to consider this lack of symmetry in the distribution of the valuations by taking account of the frequencies of the classes preceding and succeeding the modal class.

We can do this by using the following formula to find the mode for grouped data:

where

$$Mode = L_m + \left(\frac{f_m - f_{m-1}}{2 f_m - f_{m-1} - f_{m+1}} \right) C$$

$$
\begin{array}{lll}
L_m & = & \text{the lower class boundary of the modal group} \\
C & = & \text{the class interval}
\end{array}
$$

f_m, f_{m-1} and f_{m+1} =   the frequencies of the modal group, the group preceding it and the group succeeding it respectively

Taking information from Table 2.3, we can put the necessary values into the formula to give:

$$Mode = 169.5 + \left(\frac{11 - 5}{22 - 5 - 10} \right) \times 10$$

$$= 169.5 + 8.57$$

$$= £178.07$$

As f_{m+1} was much greater than f_{m-1} here, the modal value is deemed to be closer to the upper class boundary than the lower one.

2.6   OTHER AVERAGES

There are two other types of mean, which are, in certain specific situations, appropriate types of average. These are:

The geometric mean: This average is mainly used in situations where relative values are compared in a ratio form, particularly with index numbers.

The geometric mean of n numbers is the nth root of their product e.g. the geometric mean of 1, 3, 4 and 15 is $\sqrt[4]{(1 \times 3 \times 4 \times 15)} = 3.66$.

The geometric mean is less than the arithmetic mean in this example and the fact that it is not as affected by abnormal values is one reason why it is sometimes preferred to the arithmetic mean.

The harmonic mean: This average can be described as the reciprocal of the arithmetic mean of the reciprocals of the items.

The harmonic mean of 1, 2 and 3 is:

$$\frac{3}{^1/_1 + {}^1/_2 + {}^1/_3} = 1.64$$

This type of mean is only applicable in very special cases, and is only included in this section to complete the list of averages.

31

2.7 A COMPARISON OF THE ARITHMETIC MEAN, MEDIAN AND MODE

The main purpose of all these types of average is to describe the centre of a set of data, but each of them performs this function in a different, specific way.

The question of which average should be used in a given situation is not an easy one to answer.

Generally speaking, the arithmetic mean is the most important of these measures because it is the most commonly understood average and also because of its suitability for further statistical work. To calculate the mean, all the data must be utilised; whereas this is not the case with the other two measures.

The main merit of the median is that it is an average not affected by high or low value items; whereas the mean can give a distorted view of a set of data where even just one or two items lie outside the main body of values.

If we look at a simple example, the following figures show the number of storeys of ten commercial buildings in a particular area.

$$2 \quad 2 \quad 2 \quad 3 \quad 3 \quad 3 \quad 3 \quad 3 \quad 9 \quad 10$$

The mean height = 40/10 = 4 storeys.

It is fairly obvious that this is not a 'good' average to choose in this situation as it could not reasonably be judged to be representative of the data. There is not a single building with that number of storeys. Eight out of ten buildings have less storeys than this and it is only the heights of the two untypically tall buildings which drag the mean value up to that level. The median height of three storeys on the other hand is much more representative of the typical building height as it is unaffected by the two 'abnormal' values.

The mode has the major advantage of being an actual value in a set of data, whereas the mean value may not, but is less useful as an average when a set of data is widely dispersed with no obvious modal point or with more than one modal point.

Overall the arithmetic mean is the most useful statistic to represent central tendency.

2.8 QUARTILES, DECILES AND PERCENTILES

So far we have considered only measures of central location, i.e. measures which give us information on the centre of a set of data.

The median value is that which divides a group of items into two equal parts. In many circumstances, though, we may be more concerned with finding such things as the value above which three quarters of the items lie or the value below which 90 per cent of the values can be found etc.

Quartiles: If we wish to divide a set of data into four equal parts, then we find the quartile values.

The lower quartile (Q_1) is the value below which one quarter of the items lie and the upper quartile (Q_3) divides the data, such that three quarters of the items fall below it and one quarter above.

The remaining quartile (Q_2) does not have to be separately defined because it is equivalent to the median.

Decile and percentiles: Deciles are defined as those values which divide a set of items into ten equal parts. Similarly, the percentile points divide the data into a hundred equal parts.

These measures are frequently used whenever it is required that a set of data needs to be divided up into certain fixed proportions. For instance, in the example on surveying examination marks, the pass mark may be set according to the requirement that 60 per cent of the students pass the examination and 40 per cent fail. The fortieth percentile (fourth decile) therefore needs to be found.

The procedure for finding any of these above measures of location is exactly the same as the one explained for finding the median.

2.9   EXERCISES

1.   In a painting test the area covered by 500ml of primer was measured in square metres. The results of fifty such tests were

Area (mid point)	4.6	4.7	4.8	4.9	5.0	5.1	Total
Frequency	2	7	17	15	6	3	50

Calculate the arithmetic mean of the above data. Find two other averages for the data either by calculation or graphically. Discuss the advantages and disadvantages of these averages, then state, with reasons, which gives the best one for the data.

2.   The earnings of seventy-two workers on a building site are shown below:

Wage (£)	Number of Workers
181 - 190	12
191 - 200	14
201 - 210	22
211 - 220	17
221 - 230	4
231 - 240	2
241 - 250	1

Using graphical methods estimate the median wage. Comment on the use of the median to interpret this data and the reasons why it may be preferable to the mean in this case.

3

MEASURES OF DISPERSION

3.1   INTRODUCTION

The different averages dealt with so far, sum up certain characteristics of a set of data. An average value is a typical value and is often the most important statistic used to describe data.

To give a more complete description of the data we are dealing with, though, we need to consider the spread or dispersion of the data.

To show the importance of finding a measure of the dispersion of the items in a set of data, refer to Table 3.1, which shows the numbers of bricks laid by two teams of bricklayers during a certain time period.

Table 3.1: Bricks laid by two teams

Worker Number	Team A: Number of Bricks Laid	Team B: Number of Bricks Laid
1	80	96
2	91	99
3	98	100
4	111	102
5	120	103

For both teams the mean number of bricks laid is 100 but the groups are far from identical; the first group of numbers having a much greater spread than the second.

In situations such as this we need some statistic which will indicate such differences.

The main measures of dispersion are:

- (a)   the range
- (b)   the quartile deviation
- (c)   the mean deviation
- (d)   the standard deviation

We can look at each of these in turn.

3.2   THE RANGE

This is the most straightforward measure of dispersion.   We calculate the range simply by subtracting the lowest item from the highest.

In our example the range for Team A is 120 - 80 = 40 and for Team B it is 103 -96 = 7.   If this statistic were given along with the mean, it would indicate the obvious difference between the two sets of data.   The range is the easiest measure of dispersion to understand and the simplest to obtain, but as it ignores the majority of data and does not tell us anything about the dispersion between the lowest and highest values, it is considered to be a fairly crude statistic.

3.3   THE QUARTILE DEVIATION

The quartiles may be employed to arrive at a measure of dispersion.   This measure is known as the quartile deviation and is obtained by halving the inter-quartile range i.e. the difference between the lower and upper quartiles.

It can be written as:

$$Quartile\ deviation = \frac{Q_3 - Q_1}{2}$$

Whilst it is true that the quartile deviation is not affected by extreme variations -a disadvantage of the range as a measure of dispersion - the fact that the first and last quarters of the data are ignored means that it is not a satisfactory measure of the dispersion of the whole data.

As it is important to know the spread of all the items in the data, other measures are therefore used.

3.4   THE MEAN DEVIATION

This is a measure which makes use of all the data and is a statistically more satisfactory method than the range and quartile deviation.

The mean deviation gives the mean of the deviations of items from the arithmetic mean, median or mode.   (It is usually more important to calculate the mean

36

deviation of the items from the arithmetic mean because this is the 'average' most useful for further statistical work.)

The reason why we are interested in the mean deviation from the arithmetic mean is that the dispersion of a set of data will be small if the items deviate in value from the arithmetic mean by only a small amount, but deviations will be large if the items are widely dispersed in value.

The calculation of the mean deviation (from the arithmetic mean) is illustrated in Table 3.2, which relates to the data on students' surveying marks. The mean mark is 53.1.

Table 3.2: Calculation of mean deviation

Mark	Midpoint	f	*Deviation of Midpoint from Mean of 53.1* $(x - \overline{x})$	$f(x - \overline{x})$
0 - 9	4.5	1	48.6	48.6
10 - 19	14.5	2	38.6	77.2
20 - 29	24.5	4	28.6	114.4
30 - 39	34.5	4	18.6	74.4
40 - 49	44.5	7	8.6	60.2
50 - 59	54.5	15	1.4	21.0
60 - 69	64.5	9	11.4	102.6
70 - 79	74.5	3	21.4	64.2
80 - 89	84.5	2	31.4	62.8
90 - 99	94.5	3	41.4	124.2
		$\Sigma f = 50$		$\Sigma f(x - \overline{x}) = 749.6$

We are interested in the deviations of the marks from this arithmetic mean and so the fourth column shows the deviation of each midpoint from 53.1 and this is shown as $(x - \overline{x})$. In the final column these deviations are multiplied by the frequency associated with each class and the products then summed.

So we have the sum of the deviations:

$$\Sigma f(x - \overline{x}) = 749.6$$

37

To find the mean of the deviations we divide by $\Sigma f(=n)$ to give:

$$Mean\ deviation = \frac{\Sigma f(x-\overline{x})}{\Sigma f} = \frac{749.6}{50}$$

$$= 14.99 \text{ marks}$$

In this calculation the signs of the deviation (+ or -) were ignored i.e. negative signs were not used when the midpoint value was less than the mean value. The reason for this is obvious when the last column of Table 3.2 is considered.

If the first five values in the deviation column had their negative signs inserted, the first five values in the $f(x - \overline{x})$ column would have totalled - 374.8. This would have exactly matched the positive total of the last five values in the $f(x - \overline{x})$ column.

The deviations would obviously always total zero if the signs were included. The fact that the signs of the deviations are discarded is one of the reasons why the mean deviation is considered to be rather an artificial measure and unsuitable for further statistical work.

In practice, the most useful measure of dispersion for statistical work is the standard deviation which involves an approach similar to that of the mean deviation but does not include the drawbacks associated with the latter measure.

3.5   THE STANDARD DEVIATION

3.5.1 *Introduction*

This measure, which is by far the most important measure of dispersion, is basically a modification of the calculation of the mean deviation which incorporates two extra steps.

Instead of ignoring the signs of the deviations, the deviations are squared, which removes that problem. The squared deviations are added together and the total is divided by the number of items. The result is termed the **variance**.

The square root of the variance is the standard deviation.

This can be written as:

$$Standard\ deviation = \sqrt{\frac{\Sigma(x-\overline{x})^2}{n}}$$

A simple illustration on the calculation of the standard deviations can be given if we consider the earlier example on the number of bricks laid by the first team of bricklayers.

The method is shown in Table 3.3

Table 3.3: Calculation of standard deviation

Worker number	Team A Number of bricks laid	Deviation from mean of 100 $(x - \overline{x})$	$(x - \overline{x})$
1	80	-20	400
2	91	- 9	81
3	98	- 2	4
4	111	11	121
5	120	20	400
			$\Sigma(x - \overline{x})^2 = 1006$

We have already found the mean to be 100.

The total sum of the squared deviations is 1006 and so the variance is given by this total divided by the number of workers

$$Variance = \frac{\Sigma(x-\overline{x})^2}{n} = \frac{1006}{5} = 201.2$$

$$Standard\ deviation = \sqrt{\frac{\Sigma(x-\overline{x})^2}{n}} = \sqrt{201.2} = 14.18$$

39

3.5.2 *Calculating the standard deviation from a frequency distribution*

To find the standard deviation of data in a frequency table we use the same procedure as in the previous example but we need to take account of the frequencies.

The formula for finding the standard deviation from a frequency table is:

$$Standard\ deviation = \sqrt{\frac{\Sigma f(x-\overline{x})^2}{\Sigma f}}$$

Table 3.4 shows how the standard deviation can be calculated from the frequency table of students' surveying marks.

Inserting the necessary values for the formula, we obtain:

$$Standard\ deviation = \sqrt{\frac{20202}{50}} = \sqrt{404.04} = 20.1\ marks$$

Table 3.4: Calculation of standard deviation from frequency table

Mark	Midpoint	f	$(x - \overline{x})$	$(x - \overline{x})^2$	$f(x - \overline{x})^2$
0 - 09	4.5	1	-48.6	2361.96	2361.96
10 - 19	14.5	2	-38.6	1489.96	2979.92
20 - 29	24.5	4	-28.6	817.96	3271.84
30 - 39	34.5	4	-18.6	345.96	1383.84
40 - 49	44.5	7	-8.6	73.96	517.72
50 - 59	54.5	15	1.4	1.96	29.40
60 - 69	64.5	9	11.4	129.96	1169.64
70 - 79	84.5	3	21.4	457.96	1373.88
80 - 89	84.5	2	31.4	985.96	1971.92
90 - 99	94.5	3	41.4	1713.96	5141.88
		$\Sigma f = 50$			20202.00

3.5.3 Calculation of the standard deviation by the assumed mean method

The calculation involved in finding the standard deviation from a frequency table can be quite complicated even with the use of a calculator.

To simplify the arithmetical work, a method based on the use of an assumed mean can be employed. This method is also suitable in a situation where it is desired to find the standard deviation of a set of data but not necessary to find the arithmetic mean to start with.

In the surveying marks example, we might take an assumed mean of 54.5. We would then use the formula for the standard deviation taking deviations from 54.5 and make an adjustment for the difference between the assumed mean and the true mean.

As we saw in the previous chapter, the mean of the deviations of the x values ($\Sigma fd/\Sigma f$) was used to adjust the assumed mean to the true mean, when we were using this method to find the mean.

We can incorporate this into our standard deviation formula by using the square of this adjustment.

This means that the formula for the standard deviation using this method is:

$$\text{Standard deviation} = \sqrt{\frac{\Sigma d^2 f}{\Sigma f} - \left(\frac{\Sigma df}{\Sigma f}\right)^2}$$

where d = the deviation of each x value from the assumed mean.

The method can be illustrated by Table 3.5, where another simplification is made as the deviation figures are divided by 10 initially in order to reduce the arithmetic required.

41

Table 3.5:   Calculation of standard deviation using assumed mean method

Mark	Midpoint	f	Deviation from assumed mean of 54.5 in 10s d	df	d^2	d^2f
0 - 9	4.5	1	-5	- 5	25	25
10 - 19	14.5	2	-4	- 8	16	32
20 - 29	24.5	4	-3	-12	9	36
30 - 39	34.5	4	-2	- 8	4	16
40 - 49	44.5	7	-1	- 7	1	7
50 - 59	54.5	15	0	0	0	0
60 - 69	64.5	9	1	9	1	9
70 - 79	74.5	3	2	6	4	12
80 - 89	84.5	2	3	6	4	18
90 - 99	94.5	3	4	12	16	48
				$\Sigma df = -7$		$\Sigma d^2f = 203$

The formula we need to use here is therefore:

$$Standard\ deviation = C \sqrt{\frac{\Sigma d^2 f}{\Sigma f} - \left(\frac{\Sigma df}{\Sigma f}\right)^2}$$

where C = the class interval.

Putting the appropriate values into the formula:

$$Standard\ deviation = 10 \sqrt{\frac{203}{50} - \left(\frac{-7}{50}\right)^2}$$

$$= 10 \times \sqrt{(4.06 - 0.0196)}$$

$$= 10 \sqrt{4.0404}$$

$$= 20.1\ marks$$

42

So we have arrived at exactly the same answer as we did under the ordinary method, but have somewhat reduced the arithmetic involved.

3.5.4 A note on the formula for the standard deviation

One important context in which a calculation of the standard deviation of a set of data is made, occurs when an attempt is being made to make inferences about a population of items from a sample.

We can define a population as a complete set of individual objects or measurements e.g. all the houses in a particular area, all the bricks produced by a manufacturer etc. A sample, on the other hand, includes only some of the houses in an area or some of the bricks produced by a manufacturer.

How this distinction affects the formula for the standard deviation is that if we know that we are calculating the standard deviation from sample data, the denominator of the formula should be n - 1 (or Σf - 1) replacing n (or Σf).

The formula for raw data would therefore become:

$$Standard\ deviation = \sqrt{\frac{\Sigma(x - \overline{x})^2}{(n - 1)}}$$

For data in a frequency table:

$$Standard\ deviation = \sqrt{\frac{\Sigma f(x - \overline{x})^2}{\Sigma f - 1}}$$

So in situations where it is indicated that the data is sample data, the above modified formulae should be used.   Using (n - 1) is important when n is small but if n is large (say more than 100) the difference between using (n - 1) and n would be negligible.

3.6   THE COEFFICIENT OF VARIATION

One main purpose of finding a measure of dispersion for different sets of data is to enable comparisons of the variation in distributions to be made.

The standard deviation is measured in absolute terms but it can be converted to a relative form termed the coefficient of variation. This is defined as:

Coefficient of variation = standard deviation
                                          mean

or commonly as:

Coefficient of variation = 100 x standard deviation %
                                          mean

The standard deviation is expressed either as a fraction or a percentage of the mean and thus becomes a relative measure of dispersion.

We can consider an example of two distributions with the same variable but different means and standard deviations.

Example 3.1:

The mean price of houses sold in a particular year in Area A was £63 000 with a standard deviation of £9 975, whereas the mean price in B was £67 500 with a standard deviation of £10 125.

$$Coefficient\ of\ variation(Area\ A) = \frac{100\ x\ 9\ 975\%}{63\ 000}\% = 15.83\%$$

$$Coefficient\ of\ variation(Area\ B) = \frac{100\ x\ 10\ 125}{67\ 500}\% = 15.00\%$$

Thus property prices in Area A were relatively more variable than in Area B.

3.7 A NOTE ON THE INTERPRETATION OF THE STANDARD DEVIATION

A proper understanding of this most important measure can only really be gained by looking at its relationship to the normal distribution. We shall do this in the next chapter.

3.8   SKEWNESS

Having dealt with the need to provide information on the dispersion of data in addition to an average value, there may be situations where, to provide an adequate description of a set of data, an additional type of statistic is required.

This additional statistic is a measure of the symmetry or skewness of a distribution.

It is possible that two distributions could have identical means and standard deviations yet differ greatly in their appearance.

The two distributions depicted by the frequency polygons in Figure 3.1 both have a mean of 3.5 and a standard deviation of 1.2, yet the first one is perfectly symmetrical and the second one is skewed.

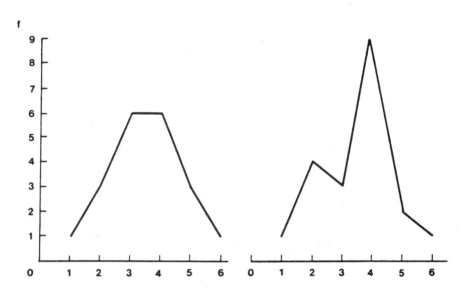

Fig 3.1: (a) Symmetrical distribution   *(b)* skew distribution

The way in which we can measure the degree of skewness of a distribution is to base the method on the fact that the greater the lack of symmetry in a distribution the greater will be the divergence between the mean, the median and the mode values. Figure 3.2 illustrates this point.

Figure 3.2(a) This frequency curve is *symmetrical* and the mean, mode and median values are all exactly equal.

Figure 3.2(b) Here the frequency curve tails off to the right and the mean value is higher than the mode and median values.   We say that the distribution is *positively skewed*.

45

Figure 3.2(c) The frequency curve tails off to the left and the mean value is less than the mode and median values. The distribution is *negatively skewed*.

A measure which shows the relative degree of skewness of a distribution is Pearson's coefficient of skewness.

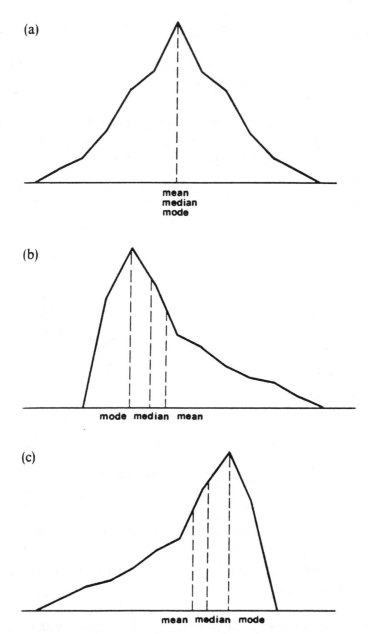

Fig 3.2: (a) Symmetrical distribution; (b) positively skewed distribution; (c) negatively skewed distribution

The formula for this coefficient is:

The main problem with using this formula is that it involves the mode, and as we

46

$$Skewness = \frac{mean - mode}{standard\ deviation}$$

saw in the previous chapter, the mode is often difficult or impossible to find.

So an alternative form of the formula is more commonly used.

For moderately skewed distributions such as those in Figure 3.2(b) and (c), the median tends to be about twice as far from the mode as from the mean i.e.

median - mode = 2(median - mean)

∴   mode = 3 median - 2 mean

Substituting this into the numerator of the formula gives

mean - 3 median + 2 mean

= 3(mean - median)

Thus the alternative formula is:

$$Skewness = \frac{3\,(mean - median)}{standard\ deviation}$$

If a distribution is perfectly symmetrical the Pearsonian coefficient will be zero e.g. For the distribution in Figure 3.1(a) the mean = 3.5, the median = 3.5 and the standard deviation = 1.2

Therefore:

$$Skewness = \frac{3\,(3.5 - 3.5)}{1.2} = 0$$

If a distribution is skew though, the direction of the skewness will determine the sign of the coefficient (+ or -) e.g. for the distribution in Figure 3.1(b), the median (4.0) is greater than the mean (3.5) and so the distribution is negatively skew.

An alternative measure of skewness may be used if previous work on a set of data

47

has already involved the calculation of the median and the quartiles. It is based on the fact that in a skew distribution the quartiles are not equidistant from the median.

The quartile on the skew side is pulled more in that direction, than is the other quartile in the opposite direction.

The relative measure of skewness is found by dividing the sum of the quartiles less twice the median by the quartile deviation i.e:

$$Skewness = \frac{Q_3 + Q_1 - 2\ median}{(Q_3 - Q_1)/2}$$

$$= \frac{2(Q_3 + Q_1 - 2\ median)}{Q_3 - Q_1}$$

3.9   EXERCISES

1.   80 students sat examinations in building technology and in construction.
     The marks were distributed as follows:

Marks	Number of Students	
	Building Technology	Construction
1 - 10	1	0
11 - 20	3	1
21 - 30	5	1
31 - 40	7	11
41 - 50	12	13
51 - 60	21	30
61 - 70	18	12
71 - 80	8	11
81 - 90	4	1
91 - 100	1	0

Calculate the mean and standard deviation of each frequency table and
compare the spread of marks in each examination

2.   A branch of a building society has 900 customers who have bought property
     within certain price ranges.   The frequency distribution of these prices is
     shown below.

Price Range (£)	Number of Customers
40 000 - 44 999	24
45 000 - 49 999	38
50 000 - 54 999	110
55 000 - 59 999	154
60 000 - 64 999	290
65 000 - 69 999	142
70 000 - 74 999	68

Find the median price and an appropriate measure of dispersion.

3.   A survey was carried out to measure the distance travelled each day from home to work.   The results, in kilometres, are tabulated below.

Distance (mid-point)	1	3	5	7	9	11	13	15	17	19
Frequency	2	4	9	18	21	19	17	7	2	1

Calculate the arithmetic mean and the standard deviation of the above data.

Use the data to draw the cumulative frequency graph and use this graph to find another average.   Give both the name and the value of this average. Use the data to draw the cumulative frequency graph and use this graph to find another average.   Give both the name and the value of this average.

What percentage of the sample travel more than 15 km to work?

4

PROBABILITY AND THE NORMAL DISTRIBUTION

4.1   PROBABILITY

The term probability is a difficult one to define in simple terms.   In statistical work we are mainly concerned with the problem of obtaining a numerical measure of probability and there are two ways of approaching this type of problem.

4.1.1   *The theoretical approach*

This can best be considered by reference to games of chance.   If we look at the simple example of throwing an unbiased die, there are six possible outcomes i.e. obtaining a one, two, three, four, five or six when the die is thrown and each outcome is equally likely to occur.   So the probability of throwing a six, P(six) - or indeed any other number - can be reasoned to be 1/6, which was deductively calculated by:

$$P \text{ (six)} = \frac{\text{Number of outcomes involving a six}}{\text{Total number of possible outcomes}}$$

This probability of 1/6 is sometimes termed the relative frequency of obtaining a six. In an example where all outcomes have an equal chance of occurring, the probability of a particular event is the number of outcomes favourable (m) to that event divided by the total number of possible outcomes (n).

$$P \text{ (event)} = \frac{m}{n}$$

We can also say that the probability that an event does not occur is (n - m)/n and in our example:

$$P \text{ (not throwing a six)} = P(\text{one, two, three, four or five}) = 5/6$$

Thus total probability i.e. the sum of the probabilities of all possible outcomes, equals one. This is termed *certainty*.

$$P \text{ (six)} + P \text{ (not obtaining a six)} = 1/6 + 5/6 = 1$$

One of these two events is certain to occur.

1 is an extreme value of probability, the other extreme being 0. If P(event) =0, the event is an *impossibility*.

4.1.2 *The empirical approach*

This involves a study of how often an event occurs in a large number of trials.

Expected relative frequencies can be applied in situations such as tossing a coin, throwing a die etc. but not in many real life situations. It may be necessary to derive expected relative frequencies from empirical findings.

For example, a random sample of 100 students at a college may show that ten of the students have blond hair. So we could estimate that the proportion of all the students in the college with blond hair is 1 in 10 and thus state that the probability of any student chosen at random having blond hair is:

$$\frac{1}{10}$$

4.2 THE RULES OF PROBABILITY

There are two basic rules which can be applied to probability. The first is the addition rule. If there are two or more ways in which an event can occur, then as long as the separate ways are *mutually exclusive* (i.e. two or more cannot occur simultaneously) the probability of its occurring is the sum of the probabilities of each of the different ways.
Thus the probability of obtaining a five or six when a die is thrown is (1/6 + 1/6) = 1/3.

If we are concerned with the probability of two or more events occurring simultaneously or in succession, then the multiplication rule must be used.

The rule is that the probability of the occurrence of such events is the product of the separate probabilities of each event.

The probability of obtaining two sixes when two dice are thrown is (1/6 × 1/6) = 1/36.

The two events - obtaining a six on one die and obtaining a six on the second die - are termed *independent events*, because the occurrence of one event in no way affects the occurrence of the other.

If events are non-independent, adjustments to the probabilities used need to be made. If we are concerned with the probability of obtaining two aces when a pack of cards is cut twice, then the probability of choosing an ace initially is 4/52 (or 1/13) and if an ace is chosen and then returned to the pack and a choice from fifty two cards is again made, the probability of a second ace is also 1/13. We therefore have two independent events and the probability of choosing two aces is (1/13 x 1/13) = 1/169.

However, if the initial ace chosen had not been returned to the pack, the probability of choosing a second ace from the fifty one remaining cards must be 3/51 (or 1/17) as only three aces are left. This probability of 1/17 is termed a *conditional probability*. So now the probability of choosing two aces is (1/13 × 1/17) = 1/221.

Example 4.1

There are 200 dwellings in a certain village and they can be classified as follows:

Type of Dwelling	Small (two bedrooms)	Medium-sized (three bedrooms)	Large (four or more bedrooms)
Terraced	32	24	4
Semi-detached	10	68	32
Detached	2	12	16

If an interviewer conducting a survey chooses a dwelling at random, find the probability that it is:

(a)   a large or medium-sized detached;
(b)   a small or medium-sized dwelling.

If two dwellings are chosen at the same time, find the probability that:

(c)   both are large dwellings;
(d)   they are both either medium-sized terraced or both large terraced;
(e)   they are of different size.

The probability of choosing a particular category of dwelling is given by:

<u>Number in that category</u>
Total number of dwellings

e.g. P (a large detached)   =   <u>Number of large detached</u>
Number of dwellings

$$= 16/200 = 0.08$$

When one dwelling only is chosen, the events considered are mutually exclusive, so the addition rule applies.

So we can find:

(a)   P (a large or medium sized detached)

= P (a large detached) + P (a medium-sized detached)

= 16/200 + 12/200 = 0.14

(b)   P (a small or medium-sized dwelling) = 44/200 + 104/200 = 0.74

(c)   When two dwellings are chosen at the same time, conditional probabilities are involved and the multiplication rule applies.

P (two large dwellings)

=   P (a large dwelling) × P (a large dwelling once one has already been chosen)

=   52/200 × 51/199 = 0.0667

(d)   This involves the addition rule too.   We need to find:

P (two medium-sized terraced) + P (two large terraced)

= (24/200 × 23/199) + (4/200 × 3/199) = 0.0142

(e)   P (two of different size) = 1 - [P (two small dwellings)
        + P (two medium-sized dwellings) + P (two large dwellings)]

        = 1 - [(44/200 × 43/199) + (104/200 × 103/199) + (52/200 × 51/199)]
        = 0.6167

4.3   PERMUTATIONS AND COMBINATIONS

Permutations   A permutation is simply an arrangement of objects.   For instance, if there are 9 students in a certain class and there are 4 desks in the front row, how many different arrangements of students in the front seats are possible?

There are 9 students who could fill the first seat, 8 who could have the second, 7 the third and 6 the final one.   So the number of ways of filling the four seats is 9 × 8 × 7 × 6 = 3024.
This is the number of permutations of 9 items taken 4 at a time.   It is written as P_4^9.

In general we wish to find the number of arrangements of r from n and this is given by

$$P_r^n = \frac{n!}{(n - r)!}$$

where n! (called n factorial) = n × (n - 1) × (n - 2) ×...× 1 and (n - r)! = (n - r) × (n -r -1) × (n - r - 2) ×...× 1

e.g. $P_4^9 = \dfrac{9 \times 8 \times 7 \times 6 \times 5 \times 4 \times 3 \times 2 \times 2}{5 \times 4 \times 3 \times 2 \times 1} = 3024$

as already shown.

Combinations   A combination of objects is a selection of n objects taken r at a time without regard to the order in which they are selected.

The formula for a combination is

$$C_r^n = \frac{n!}{r!(n - r)!}$$

So if we wished to know the number of ways in which a sub-committee consisting of 2 people could be chosen from a committee of 6 people we could find the answer from

$$C_2^6 = 6!/2!4! = \frac{6 \times 5 \times 4 \times 3 \times 2 \times 1}{(2 \times 1) \times (4 \times 3 \times 2 \times 1)} = 15 \text{ ways}$$

4.4 THE BINOMIAL DISTRIBUTION

A binomial distribution, as the name suggests, is concerned with two possible events occurring. For example, if a coin is tossed it will either come down heads or tails. The formula used for combinations and the multiplication rule can be used together to consider the distribution of probabilities when we have such events.
If p is the probability of obtaining a head when a coin is tossed and q is the probability of obtaining a tail, then when a coin is tossed twice the various possible outcomes are: two heads, one head then one tail, one tail then one head, or two tails.

The probabilities of these outcomes being given by p^2, pq, qp and q^2 respectively. As these are the only possible outcomes, these probabilities must total 1, i.e.

$$p^2 + 2pq + q^2 = 1$$

This is the expansion of $(p + q)^2$.

If the coin were tossed n times then the probabilities of the various outcomes would be given by the terms of the expansion of $(p + q)^n$.

This is:

$$(p + q)^n = p^n + C_1^n p^{n-1} q + C_2^n p^{n-2}q^2 + \dots C_r^n p^{n-r} q^r + \dots + C_n^n q^n$$

where the term $C_r^n p^{n-r} q^r$ = the probability of obtaining (n - r) heads and r tails in n tosses of the coin.

For example, if a coin is tossed 6 times the probability of obtaining 4 heads is:

$$\frac{6 \times 5 \times 4 \times 3 \times 2 \times 1}{(4 \times 3 \times 2 \times 1) \times (2 \times 1)} \left(\frac{1}{2}\right)^2 \left(\frac{1}{2}\right)^4 = 0.234$$

This formula can be used even when p and q are not equal. Generally, the mean of a binomial distribution is the number of times (n) an experiment (e.g. tossing a coin) is carried out times the probability (p) of a success (e.g. obtaining a head) = np. The standard deviation is √npq.

Situations, though, where p and q are both equal are the most interesting. If a coin were tossed 1000 times and the probability of obtaining every possible number of heads from zero to 1000 were calculated, then the frequency curve formed by smoothing a set of histogram blocks depicting the probabilities could be formed as shown in Figure 4.1.

An important feature of this curve is that it is symmetrical about the mean. Its significance will become apparent in the following sections on the normal distribution.

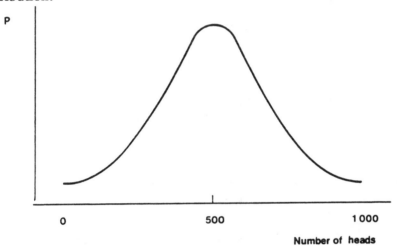

Fig 4.1: Distribution of probabilities showing the number of heads obtained from 1000 tosses of a coin.

4.5 THE NORMAL DISTRIBUTION

It is important when dealing with data to know whether we are dealing with aggregate population data or just a sample i.e. a part of the population.

When finding the mean or standard deviation of sample data we are finding a *statistic*. The mean and standard deviation of the population are called *parameters*. The distinction is important because the parameters of a population, which includes all possible items, are fixed whereas the statistics obtained from sample data vary according to which items make up the sample.

It is the theoretical distribution of a population with which we are concerned in this chapter.

The notation used to denote the mean and standard deviation of a population differs from that used for sample statistics. Greek letters are used to denote population parameters. The population mean is denoted by μ (pronounced mu) as against the sample mean of x.

The population standard deviation is σ (pronounced sigma) compared to the sample standard deviation denoted by s.

4.6   THE NORMAL CURVE

The *normal distribution* (or normal frequency curve) is a theoretical frequency distribution which is of fundamental importance in statistical theory.

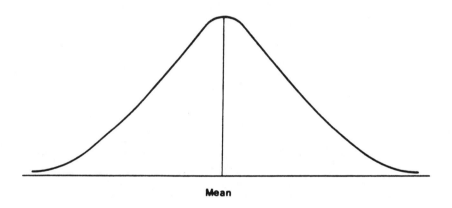

Fig 4.2:   Typical normal curve

The actual shape of any normal curve depends upon the mean and standard deviation of the population which it depicts.

This can be seen from the equation of a normal curve whose mean is μ, and standard deviation is σ.   It is

$$y = \frac{1}{\sqrt{2\pi . \sigma^2}} . e^{-\frac{1}{2}((x-\mu)/\sigma)^2}$$

So if we know the mean and standard deviation of a population we can insert a value for x to find y, i.e. the height of the curve.

Figure 4.3 shows how two normal distributions can differ in appearance even if they have the same means, but have different standard deviations.

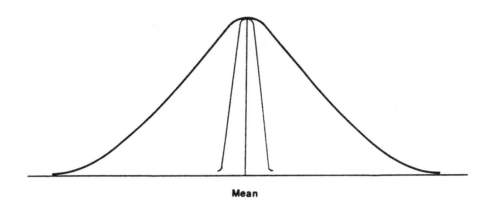

Fig 4.3: Two normal curves with same means but different standard deviations.

To make the normal curve a more useful tool of statistical analysis, it is possible to standardise any normal curve to produce a standard normal distribution.

4.7   THE SIGNIFICANCE OF THE NORMAL DISTRIBUTION

The most important feature of a normal distribution is that the area under the normal curve relates to the proportion of items holding values between two points on the horizontal scale.

For instance, 68.26 per cent of the area of a normal curve lies between the points one standard deviation either side of the mean.   Figure 4.4 illustrates the areas found between points one and two standard deviations respectively either side of the mean.

If it is known then that an item is normally distributed and the mean and standard deviation values are given, the proportion of the values falling between any two chosen values can be calculated.

To undertake such calculations in practice the task is simplified by the fact that any normal distribution can be converted into a standard normal distribution.   The advantage of this is that statistical tables are produced which show the areas under a standard normal curve which fall between certain values.

4.8   THE STANDARD NORMAL DISTRIBUTION

This is a version of the normal distribution which has a mean $(\mu) = 0$ and a standard deviation $(\sigma) = 1$.

The usefulness of the standard normal distribution is that the values in any normal distribution can be converted to values in the standardised version and these converted values looked up in a standard normal distribution table.   This conversion is undertaken by changing the scale of the normal distribution.

A value x on the scale of a normal distribution with a mean μ and a standard deviation σ has a corresponding z value on the scale of the standard normal distribution of

$$z = \frac{x - \mu}{\sigma}$$

The resulting z value is called the standard score.

The relationship between the x scale of a normal distribution and the z scale is shown in Figure 4.5.

So, given any value on the x scale we can convert it to the z scale and once we have converted to the z scale, the table of areas can be used.

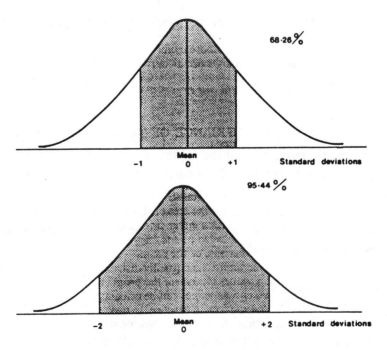

Fig 4.4:   Areas under the normal distribution curve

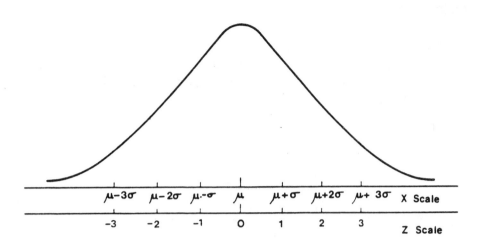

Fig 4.5: Relationship between the x scale and z scale

4.9 Z VALUES AND AREAS UNDER THE NORMAL CURVE

The area under a normal distribution curve represents all the values of the variable which can arise, and the proportion of the area under the curve between any two points on the x scale therefore represents the proportion of the items which hold values between those limits.

A table could be drawn up for any normal distribution with a specific mean and standard deviation to show such proportionate areas, but as any normal distribution can be standardised, all that is needed is a table which shows the proportionate areas under the standard normal curve. Such a table (Table 1) is shown in the Appendix. The total area under the standard normal curve is equal to 1 (or 100 per cent) as it contains all the items in the population and the table is designed to show the proportion of the area under the curve which is to be found to the left of any z value.

(It is an unfortunate fact that some statistical tables of the normal distribution are composed in a different way and might instead give the area under the curve which is to the right of the z value. The user of any normal curve table should check carefully exactly what is being measured in any table being used).

The way to use the 'z table' in the Appendix is to look down the z column to find the calculated z value and then read off the area which is given as a decimal figure in the next column.

Examples on finding areas.

1. As the mean of the standard normal distribution is 0 (see Figure 4.5) then obviously exactly 50 per cent of the area under the curve lies to the left of the mean, and so the area which corresponds to a z value of 0.00 is given as 0.5000 (i.e. 50 per cent).

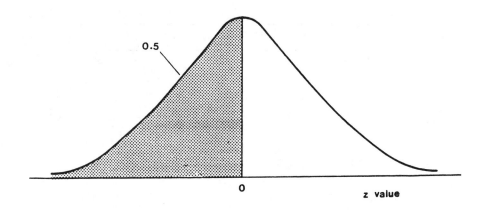

Fig 4.6: Area to the left of z = 0.00

2. For a positive z value it is a simple matter to use the z table. The area which lies to the left of the z value of 1.29 is 0.9015, which means that just over 90 per cent of the area lies to the left of 1.29.

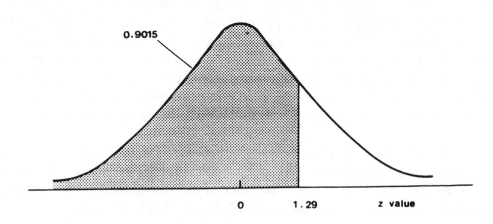

Fig 4.7: Area to the left of z = 1.29

3. If the calculated value of z is negative, the corresponding positive value can be looked up in the table, and due to the exact symmetry of the normal curve, the area to the left of this positive z value corresponds to the area to the right of the negative z value i.e. if the calculated z value is -1.29 the proportion of the area to the *right* of this value is just over 90 per cent of the total area.

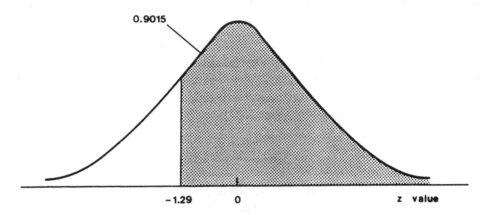

Fig 4.8: Area to the right of z = -1.29

4. Finding the proportion of the area that lies between two z values is also possible.

    Suppose we need to find the area between a z value of -0.82 and a z value of 1.66. From the table of areas, the area to the left of the z value of 1.66 is 0.9515. For the reason explained in the previous example we can find from the table the area to the right of z = -0.82. It is 0.7939. So the area to the *left* of the z value of -0.82 must be 1 - 0.7939 = 0.2061.

    Subtracting 0.2061 from 0.7939 gives 0.5878 as the shaded area in Figure 4.9, i.e. 58.78 per cent of the area lies between the z values of -0.82 and 1.66.

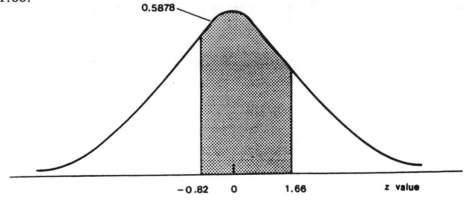

Fig 4.9: Area between z = - 0.82 and z = 1.66

63

4.10   AREAS UNDER THE NORMAL CURVE AND PROBABILITIES

To understand the use of the normal curve in the calculation of probabilities, we can relate back to section 4.4 on the binomial distribution.

Any area under the binomial curve between two points depicts the probability of obtaining values between those points and the same is true for the normal curve.

If we know that a variable is normally distributed, then the area under the curve between any two points indicates the probability of a randomly chosen item holding a value between those two points.

The following example shows this.

Example 4.2

The heights of a town's adult male population are known to be normally distributed with a mean of 1.75m and a standard deviation of 0.12m.

If an individual is chosen at random from the population, find the probability that he will be:

(a)   under 1.65m;
(b)   over 1.95m;
(c)   between 1.70m and 1.85m.

(a) $z = \dfrac{1.65 - 1.75}{0.12} = \dfrac{-0.10}{0.12} = -0.83$

We need to find the area to the left of z = -0.83 as shown in Figure 4.10(a).

From the z table, the area to the left of z = +0.83 is 0.7967.   So the area to the right of z = -0.83 is also 0.7967.   This means that the required area is (1 - 0.7967) = 0.2033.

The probability of a randomly chosen individual being under 1.65m is therefore 0.2033.

(b) $z = \dfrac{1.95 - 1.75}{0.12} = \dfrac{0.20}{0.12} = 1.67$

The area to the right of 1.67 (see Figure 4.10b) is required. From the z table, the area to the left of $z = 1.67$ is 0.9525. The required area is thus $(1 - 0.9525) = 0.0475$. This is the probability of a chosen individual being taller than 1.95m.

(c)   Here we need to find two z values. z_1 is the value which corresponds to 1.70m and z_2 relates to 1.85m.

$$z_1 \quad = \quad \frac{1.70 - 1.75}{0.12} \quad = \quad \frac{-0.05}{0.12} = \quad -0.42$$

and $$z_2 \quad = \quad \frac{1.85 - 1.75}{0.12} \quad = \quad \frac{0.10}{0.12} = \quad 0.83$$

The area we need to find is that between z_1 and z_2 (see Figure 4.10c).

From the z table, the area to the right of $z = +0.42$ is found to be 0.6628 and so the area to the right of $z = -0.42$ is also 0.6628. This means that the area to the left of $z = -0.42$ must therefore be $(1 - 0.6628) = 0.3372$.

Now the area to the left of $z = 0.83$ is given as 0.7967 in the table.

The required area i.e. that between $z_1 = -0.42$ and $z = 0.83$, must be equal to $(0.7967 - 0.3372) = 0.4595$, which is the probability that the chosen individual is between 1.70m and 1.85m.

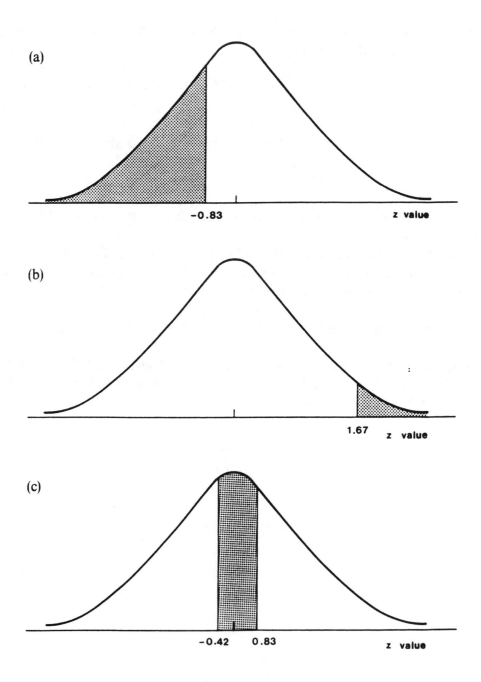

Fig 4.10:   (a) Area to the left of z = -0.83; (b) area to the right of z = 1.67; (c) area between z = -0.42 and z = 0.83

4.11 EXERCISES

1. A library contains 75 000 books of which 1 500 are relevant to quantity surveying. It also contains 1 000 journals of which twenty-five are relevant to quantity surveying. A person enters the library, selects a book at random and then looks at a journal at random. What is the probability that:

   (a) both book and journal are relevant to quantity surveying;
   (b) one is relevant but the other is not?

   While the first person is reading the journal a second person enters and picks a journal at random, what is the probability that:

   (c) both are quantity surveying journals;
   (d) neither is a quantity surveying journal?

2. From observations over a long period of time the following probabilities have been found for three machines on a building site.

	Working	Idle	Broken Down
Machine 1	0.6	0.3	0.1
Machine 2	0.7	?	0.2
Machine 3	?	0.4	0.1

   Use the laws of probability to find:

   (a) the missing values;
   (b) the probability that all machines are working;
   (c) the probability that no machines are broken down;
   (d) the probability that at least two machines are idle.

5

INDEX NUMBERS

5.1 INTRODUCTION

An index number is a measure, over time, designed to show average changes in the price, quantity or value of a group of items.

If we wish to compare several series of figures, it is more than likely that their complexity will render direct comparison meaningless. If, for instance, we had information on every form of production in the building industry during this year and last year (e.g. number of bricks produced, tonnes of cement etc), the sheer mass of data would make it impossible to see clearly in which year production was higher. Instead of such an excess of figures, what we need is a single figure, which in itself shows how much one year differs from another. A convenient way of doing this is to take a typical year's figures as a base and express the figures for other years as a measure of this. Such a single figure, summarising a comparison between the two sets of figures, is called an index number. Although it has just been stated that index numbers are mainly used to deal with a number of items, the simplest type of index number series to compile is a single item index.

5.2 SINGLE-ITEM INDEX NUMBERS

Where only one item is involved in comparisons between different periods, the calculation of index numbers is very simple. Assuming that annual data are being dealt with, one year is chosen as base and the values for the other years are stated in proportion to the value for the base year.

Example 5.1: A firm of builder's merchants has the following sales figures for a particular commodity as shown in Table 5.1.

Year	*Amount Sold (tonnes)*
1989	430
1990	472
1991	483
1992	493
1993	502
1994	510

If 1990 is chosen as the base year, then the index number for 1990 is 100, and the index number for any other year is found by dividing that year's sales figure by the 1989 sales figure and then multiplying by 100 to put the resulting proportion into index number form. This can be expressed by the notation:

$$\text{Index number for year } n = q_n/q_o \times 100$$

Where

q_o = the quantity sold in the base year (1990 here)

q_n = the quantity sold in the current year

The whole index number series can thus be calculated as in Table 5.2.

Table 5.2: Calculation for whole index number series

Year	Amount Sold (tonnes)	Index of Sales
1989	430	430/472 x 100 = 91.1
1990	472	100.0
1991	483	483/472 x 100 = 102.3
1992	493	493/472 x 100 = 104.4
1993	502	502/472 x 100 = 106.6
1994	510	510/472 x 100 = 108.0

5.3   MULTI-ITEM INDEX NUMBERS

Where more than one item is involved, a multi-item index needs to be used. This normally means the calculation of a weighted aggregative index.

Example 5.2

A firm of builder's merchants divides its commodities into four main groups and the quantities sold and its prices (£), for a three year period are as shown in Table 5.3.

Table 5.3: Quantities and prices of commodities sold by builder's merchants

Commodity	Unit	(1992)		(1993)		(1994)	
		Qty	ppu(£)	Qty	ppu(£)	Qty	ppu(£)
A	tonne	120	10.0	150	10.4	160	11.0
B	tonne	50	20.0	60	20.0	70	24.0
C	m²	1000	4.0	1200	4.2	1200	4.8
D	m³	500	4.0	700	4.6	800	5.0

(Key: Qty - Quantity; ppu(£) - price per unit (£))

The firm wishes to measure *the overall* change in prices over this period and 1992 is chosen as the base year.

In other words, the firm wishes to find one index figure for each year which shows how the prices of its products have changed in aggregate; it does not wish to produce an index for each commodity individually.

In constructing its index then, the firm must take into account the relative importance of the various commodities, e.g. the fact that much more of commodity 'C' than of commodity 'D' is sold each year, so the effect of a change in price of the former commodity will be so much greater. A weighted average must therefore be found.

The obvious weightings to take in this example are the quantities of the commodities sold. One way of doing this is to use weights which show the relative importance of the commodities in the base period, i.e. the base year quantities. Such an index is said to be 'base weighted' or of the **Laspeyres** type.

Another method is to calculate the weights using quantities consumed in the current year, and an index number of this type is described as 'current weighted' or a **Paasche** type.

These two types of index are defined as follows:

$$\text{Laspeyres price index for year n} \quad = \quad (\Sigma p_n q_0 / \Sigma p_0 q_0) \times 100$$

Where

p_n and p_0 are the current and base year prices respectively, q_n and q_0 are the respective quantities.

This index indicates how much the cost of buying base year quantities at current year prices compares with base year costs.

Paasche price index for year n $= (\Sigma p_n q_n / \Sigma p_o q_n) \times 100$

This index indicates how much current year costs are related to the cost of buying current year quantities at base year prices.

Returning to our example, we can now calculate these indices.

The calculations for the Laspeyres price index with 1992 (= 100) as base year are as follows:

$\Sigma p_{1992} q_{1992}$ $=$ (10.0 x 120) + (20.0 x 50)
+ (4.0 x 1000) + (4.0 x 500)
$=$ 8 200

$\Sigma p_{1993} q_{1992}$ $=$ (10.4 x 120) + (20.0 x 50)
+ (4.2 x 1000) + (4.6 x 500)
$=$ 8 748

$\Sigma p_{1994} q_{1992}$ $=$ (11.0 x 120) + (24.0 x 50)
+ (4.8 x 1000) + (5.0 x 500)
$=$ 9 820

The price index series for the three years is:

1992		=	100
1993	8 748/8 200 x 100	=	106.7
1994	9 820/8 200 x 100	=	119.8

Paasche price index with 1992 (= 100) as base year

$\Sigma p_{1992} q_{1993}$ $=$ (10.0 x 150) + (20.0 x 60)
+ (4.0 x 1200) + (4.0 x 700)
$=$ 10 300

$\Sigma p_{1993} q_{1993}$ $=$ (10.4 x 150) + (20.0 x 60)
+ (4.2 x 1200) + (4.6 x 700)
$=$ 11 020

71

$$\Sigma\ p_{1992}q_{1994} = \quad (10.0 \times 160) + (20.0 \times 70)$$
$$+ (4.0 \times 1200) + (4.0 \times 800)$$
$$= \quad 11\ 000$$

$$\Sigma\ p_{1994}q_{1994} = \quad (11.0 \times 160) + 24.0 \times 70)$$
$$+ (4.8 \times 1200) + (5.0 \times 800)$$
$$= \quad 13\ 200$$

The price index series for the three years is:

1992		=	100
1993	11 020/10 300 x 100	=	107.0
1994	13 200/11 000 x 100	=	120.0

5.4   COMPARISON OF LASPEYRES AND PAASCHE INDICES

The results which we obtain by each method would only differ substantially if there were any great change in the pattern of sales.

One major advantage which the Laspeyres price index has, is in the ease of computation; the denominator of the formula remains the same each period ($\Sigma p_o q_o$), whereas with the Paasche price index ($\Sigma p_o q_n$) it has to be recalculated every period. Also, as a result of this, the different years in the Laspeyres index can be directly compared with each other and not just with the base year.

The Paasche price index, on the other hand, is much more useful when the quantities of each commodity being sold each year are likely to vary to any degree.   It may well be the case, that, due to some technological advance, there is an increase in demand for a certain commodity each year, and a base quantity weighted price index would not pick this up.

5.5   PRICE RELATIVES INDEX

A price relative is simply the price of an item in one year relative to another year, again using 100 as base.

It can be depicted, using our symbols as:

$$\frac{p_n}{p_o} \times 100$$

So, in our previous example, commodity A has a price relative of $10.4/10.0 \times 100$ = 104, comparing 1993 with 1992.

If we are concerned with the compilation of a multi-item index, a composite index number can be obtained by taking a weighted average of all the price relatives with which we are concerned.

The formula for this index number is:

$$\frac{\sum \left(\frac{p_n}{p_o} \times weight \right)}{\sum weights} \times 100$$

Table 5.4: Price relatives index

Commodity	1992 Price per unit (£)	1993 Price per unit (£)	Price Relative	Weight	Price Relative x weight
A	10.0	10.4	104	6	624
B	20.0	20.0	100	5	500
C	4.0	4.2	105	20	2 100
D	4.0	4.6	115	10	1 150
				41	4 374

Index for 1993 = 4 374/41 = 106.7

This is as was previously calculated in section 5.3.

We can, for instance, find a price relatives index for 1993 for Example 5.2 using the values of sales for 1992 as relative weights. This is shown in Table 5.4.

It should be noted that the value of sales in the base year $(p_o q_o)$ should be used to formulate the weightings rather than the base year quantities sold. (The reader may wish to work out the reason for this, using the algebraic notation). The base year values of sales are:

A: £1200   B: £1000   C: £4000   D: £2000

These can be reduced to 6, 5, 20 and 10 respectively.

It is to be expected that this index gives the same result as previously.

The main use of separate calculations of price relatives is that they allow a comparison of the relative change compared with the base data for each item.

5.6   CHOICE OF BASE YEAR

With a fixed base index, it is clearly important that the base year is selected so as to provide a satisfactory standard of comparison.   A high base year value tends to detract from other years and a low one tends to make them appear higher.   For this reason an average of several years is sometimes used to form an artificial base.

As time moves on, the base may become unrealistic.   This can occur if there has been a pronounced inflationary trend in the data so that, say, the base year prices bear little relation to current prices.   This may be of little importance if we are prepared to put up with a very large index number, but in practice a conversion to a new base year may well occur.

Conversion may be made to a new year as base simply by dividing all the index numbers by the index of the new base year on the old scale and multiplying by 100.

In Example 5.1 we could change the base of the index to 1992 = 100 as shown in Table 5.5

Table 5.5:   Change of base year

Year	Present Index of Sales (1989 = 100)	New Index of Sales (1991 = 100)		
1989	91.1	91.1/104.4 x 100	=	87.3
1990	100.0	100 /104.4 x 100	=	95.8
1991	102.3	102.3/104.4 x 100	=	98.0
1992	104.4		=	100
1993	106.4	106.4/104.4 x 100	=	101.9
1994	108.0	108.0/104.4 x 100	=	103.9

A more serious objection to index number comparisons over long periods of time is that the basic circumstances change.   Even if we are dealing with what seems to be a single commodity, it rarely remains exactly the same.   Designs change and quality varies.   This applies especially if the index number relates to a number of items.

5.7   CHAIN-BASE INDEX NUMBERS

A chain-base index is simply one in which each period in the series uses the previous period as a base.

Taking Example 5.1, a chain-base index with 1989 as the initial period would be calculated as shown in Table 5.6.

Table 5.6:   Calculations for chain-base index

Year	Amount sold (tonnes)	Chain-base index
1989	430	100
1990	472	472/430 x 100 = 109.8
1991	483	483/472 x 100 = 102.3
1992	493	493/483 x 100 = 102.0
1993	502	502/493 x 100 = 101.8
1994	510	510/502 x 100 = 101.6

Such an index shows whether the rate of change is rising, falling or constant, as well as the extent of the change from year to year.   It can be seen in this example that although there is a steady rise in sales, the increase each year in relation to the total sales of previous year is falling.

The main advantage of a chain-base index is the fact that new items can be easily accommodated into the index.

5.8   USE OF INDEX NUMBERS

There are several important considerations to bear in mind when index numbers are being studied.   The purpose of the index is of overall importance.

The choice of weights for an index will obviously determine the resulting index number for each year.   As we have seen from a comparison of index numbers by the Laspeyres and Paasche methods, if the sales figures in Example 5.2 were to vary considerably from year to year, the resulting index number series under each method may differ a great deal.

Lastly the base year of the index, especially for a price index in inflationary periods, will hopefully not be so far distant that it is difficult to relate the figures back.   If this is a problem, then a rebasing might be needed.

5.9   EXERCISES

1.   (a)   Why is weighting used in the construction of index numbers? Describe how weighting is achieved with Laspeyres and Paasche prices indices.

(b)   Construct a weighted index series from the following data to show (i) the change in prices and (ii) the change in quantities

Item	Unit	Quantity			Price		
		1992	**1993**	**1994**	**1992**	**1993**	**1994**
X	m²	1000	1000	1200	6	7	9
Y	m³	400	500	600	10	12	15
Z	tonne	100	150	200	10	10	14

2.   What are the main factors to be considered in constructing an index number series?

A firm classifies its output into three types of building A, B, and C. Its records for four recent years are:

Type	1990		1991		1992		1993	
	a	*b*	*a*	*b*	*a*	*b*	*a*	*b*
A	6	120	8	168	9	198	11	264
B	10	100	12	132	16	176	20	240
C	40	240	44	286	50	315	60	387

a is the number of units.   *b* is the value in £000s.

Use the data to compile an index number series with 1990 as base year, using a weighted arithmetic mean.   The purpose of the index is to measure the overall change in quantity of buildings produced.

3. (a)   Explain the purpose of weighting in index number construction.

    (b)   Summarise the advantages and disadvantages of base-weighted and of current-weighted index numbers.

    (c)   Combine the two following index number series into a base-weighted (Laspeyres), average-of-relative type index series, based on 1991.

Mid-year	Labour Costs		Material Costs	
	Index	Weight	Index	Weight
1991	196	41	198	59
1992	238	48	236	52
1993	282	47	283	53

6

LINEAR REGRESSION

6.1 INTRODUCTION

In business or industry it is often necessary to predict trends and it is the job of the statistician has a role to play in making these predictions.

Predictions based on statistical information can only be in terms of probability but they are satisfactory if a high percentage of them prove to be correct.

We usually need to express relationships between quantities that are known and quantities that are to be predicted by using mathematical equations.

The simplest and most widely used equation for expressing such relationships is the linear equation

$$Y = a + bX$$

where a and b are constants, and if we know the values of a and b then we can predict the corresponding value for the variable Y for a given value of variable X.

6.2 A LINEAR RELATIONSHIP

If the producer of a certain product X has fixed costs of production of £10 000 and constant variable costs of £3 000 per unit of output of X, then the total cost (Y) for any level of output can be found from the equation

$$Y = £(10\ 000 + 3\ 000X)$$

So if an output of, say, 5 units of X is produced the total costs will be

$$Y = £10\ 000 + (3\ 000 \times 5)$$

$$= £25\ 000$$

This linear relationship is depicted in Figure 6.1.

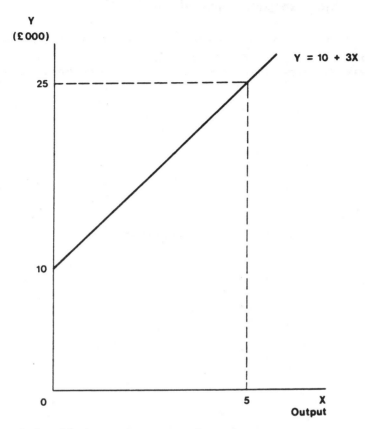

Fig 6.1: Relationship between costs and output

In many situations, though, we may have sets of values for two variables and we may believe that there is a linear relationship between the two lots of data but we do not know the value of the two parameters a and b. If we are not given the values of a and b we need some method of calculating them so as to fit appropriately the data we are given.

Example 6.1:

A supplier of building materials has information on his advertising expenditure on a certain product and also the returns from the sale of that product over the previous eight years. Using this information (shown in Table 6.1) the supplier would like to estimate his sales figure for a future year after he has decided on his advertising expenditure.

The two sets of values shown in Table 6.1 are plotted on a diagram called a **scatter diagram**, as shown in Figure 6.2.

Table 6.1: Advertising expenditure and sales returns

Year	Advertising (£00)	Sales (£0000)
1	1	1
2	3	2
3	4	4
4	6	4
5	8	5
6	9	7
7	11	8
8	14	9

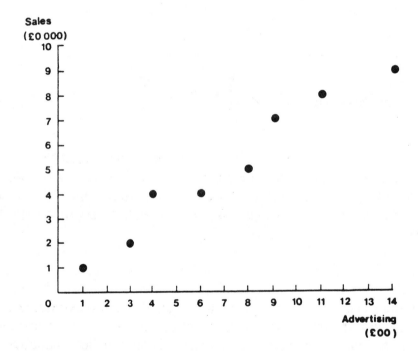

Fig 6.2: Scatter diagram of sales and advertising data

It would appear from the diagram that the relationship between these two variables may approximate to a linear one. A line can be drawn through the points as in Figure 6.3, but is only one of many that can be drawn and the problem is one of choosing which is the best line to fit to the points.

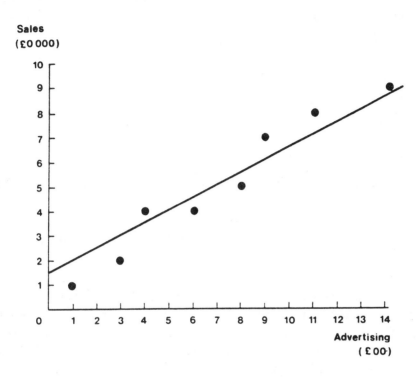

Fig 6.3: One possible line through the scattered points

6.3 THE LINE OF BEST FIT

The supplier requires a line fitted to the points, from which he is able to make the best predictions. Such a line is called the **line of best fit.** A criterion is needed on the basis of which it is possible to find this line which provides the best fit even though it does not pass through all the points. The procedure for obtaining such a line is called the **method of least squares.** This method requires that the sum of the squared vertical distances from the points to the line is at a minimum.

The basic idea underlying this method is that it is desirable that the line be useful for predictive purposes, and so, to minimise the error of prediction, it is necessary to minimise the distances between the line and the existing data points.

The reason why it is not possible to merely add together the distances by which the points deviate from the line is that obviously some of the distances between the points and the line are positive whilst others are negative. Therefore the sum of these distances could be quite small even when the deviations are large. Such problems are overcome by squaring the deviations.

6.4   THE METHOD OF LEAST SQUARES

The standard approach to this method is to work from what are called **normal equations**. These are two simultaneous equations which when solved using the sample data come up with values for the two constants a and b.

These equations are:

$$\Sigma Y = an + b\Sigma X$$
$$\text{and} \quad \Sigma XY = a\Sigma X + b\Sigma X^2$$

where n is the number of pairs of observations and ΣX, ΣY, ΣXY and ΣX^2 are calculated from the data.

These values can be substituted in the two equations which can then be solved simultaneously to give the required values of a and b.

By solving the above normal equations, the equation for the regression line of Y on X is found.   This means that the line found can suitably be used to enable the prediction of a value for Y from a known value of X.   Therefore, X is said to be the independent variable while Y is the dependent variable.   When labelling the variables it is of vital importance that this distinction is borne in mind.

A regression line of X on Y could also be found by interchanging the Xs and Ys in the normal equations and performing a separate calculation, but the two regression lines found would not be the same and one could not be obtained directly from the other.

In our example, then, the advertising figures will be the X values and the sales figures the Y values, as the supplier is trying to find an equation which will enable him to predict the level of sales, given a certain advertising expenditure.

The calculations as shown in Table 6.2 must therefore be carried out.

We have the following values:

$$\Sigma X = 56 \quad \Sigma Y = 40 \quad \Sigma X^2 = 524 \quad \Sigma XY = 364 \text{ and } n = 8.$$

Putting these values into the normal equations:

$$40 = 8a + 56b \qquad\qquad (1)$$
$$364 = 56a + 524b \qquad\qquad (2)$$

Table 6.2: Calculations for finding regression equation

Year	Advertising (£00)	Sales (£0000)	X^2	XY
1	1	1	1	1
2	3	2	9	6
3	4	4	16	16
4	6	4	36	24
5	8	5	64	40
6	9	7	81	63
7	11	8	121	88
8	14	9	256	126
	56	40	524	364

In order to eliminate the a's multiply equation (1) by 7.

$$280 = 56a + 392b \qquad (3)$$

Subtracting equation (3) from equation (2),

$$84 = 132b$$

$$\therefore \quad b = 84/132 = 0.636$$

Substituting this value for b into equation (1) gives

$$40 = 8a + (56 \times 0.636)$$

$$\therefore \quad 8a = 40 - 35.6 = 4.4$$

$$\therefore \quad a = 4.4/8 = 0.55$$

The regression equation is

$$Y = 0.55 + 0.636X$$

The regression line is shown in Figure 6.4. It can be drawn quite simply from the equation by inserting two values for X into the equation, finding the corresponding value for Y in each case, plotting the resultant points and joining the points by a straight line.

6.5   USE OF THE REGRESSION LINE FOR PREDICTION PURPOSES

Any value for X can now be substituted into the regression equation in order to give the estimated level of Y. If the X value used is within the range of values for which data already exist, then to estimate the corresponding value for Y is termed **interpolation**.

If, however, the regression line is extended and some value for X is chosen which has never been met with before, then the estimated value for Y is found by **extrapolation**.

For instance, if our supplier wished to estimate the level of sales he could expect from an expenditure of £700 on advertising, this level of expenditure lies within the existing range of advertising figures (£100 to £1400) and so the corresponding sales figure can be found by interpolation.

To find the likely level of sales associated with a higher level of advertising expenditure than he has undertaken before, e.g. £1600, extrapolation is needed.

These estimated sales figures can be found quite simply by plugging the advertising values into the regression equation.

When £700 is spent,

$$X = 7 \text{ and}$$

$$Y = 0.55 + (0.636 \times 7)$$

$$= 5.002$$

i.e. an estimated sales value of £50 020.

When £1 600 is spent

$$X = 16 \text{ and}$$

$$Y = 0.55 + (0.636 \times 16)$$

$$= 10.726$$

i.e. an estimated sales value of £107 270.

These figures could also be read off from the regression line.

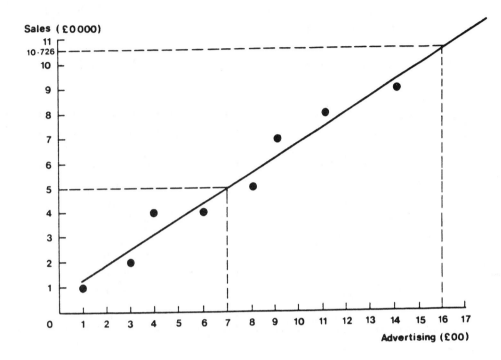

Fig 6.4: Regression line

6.6 EXERCISES

1. (a) By reference to the data in the table demonstrate how an estimate of the linear trend in construction costs could be derived.

    (b) Suggest what further analysis might be desirable in view of the results obtained.

Year	Out turn tender price indices (Private commercial)
1987	100
1988	110
1989	126
1990	158
1991	220
1992	266
1993	285
1994	305

2. A household expenditure survey produced the following data.

Income (£)	90	110	130	150	170
Housing Expenditure (£)	14.44	14.94	17.06	17.36	19.42

Assume that there is a linear relationship between the income (X) and the housing expenditure (Y) and use the data to find an equation to represent the relationship.

Use this equation to predict the housing expenditure when the income is (a) £100 and (b) £200.

7

CORRELATION

7.1 INTRODUCTION

So far we have fitted a least squares regression line to our sample observations. From the examples we have covered, the positions of the points on the graph have made it seem reasonable to fit a straight line to the points. In some cases, however, we might be doubtful as to whether predictions using a straight line fitted to the points will be a true representation and as to whether predictions using a straight line will be accurate.

It is therefore necessary to have some measure of the accuracy of fitting a straight line through out points.

7.2 SCATTER DIAGRAMS

If we take a scatter diagram (Figure 7.1)

$$\text{Let } x_i = X_i - \overline{X}$$

$$y_i = Y_i - \overline{Y}$$

In quadrant I,

$$(X_i - \overline{X}) > 0 \text{ and } (Y_i - \overline{Y}) > 0$$

$$\therefore \quad x_i y_i > 0$$

In quadrant II,

$$(X_i - \overline{X}) < 0 \text{ and } (Y_i - \overline{Y}) > 0$$

$$\therefore \quad x_i y_i < 0$$

In quadrant III,

$$(X_i - \overline{X}) < 0 \text{ and } (Y_i - \overline{Y}) < 0$$

$$\therefore \quad x_i y_i > 0$$

In quadrant IV,

$$(X_i - \overline{X}) > 0 \text{ and } (Y_i - \overline{Y}) < 0$$

$$\therefore \quad x_i y_i < 0$$

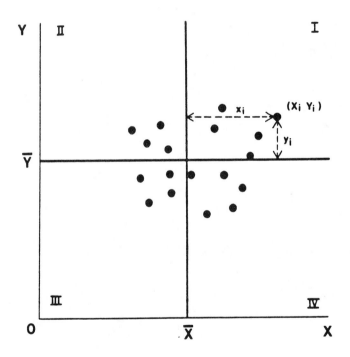

Fig 7.1: Scatter diagram

Consider the three scatter diagrams shown in Figure 7.2.

In Figure 7.2(a), as the association between X and Y is positive, most of the points lie in quadrants I and III and $\Sigma x_i y_i$ will tend to be positive.

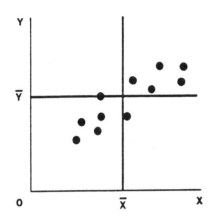

Fig 7.2(a): Positive relationship between X and Y

In Fig 7.2(b), as the association is negative, most of the points will lie in quadrants II and IV and $\Sigma x_i y_i$ will tend to be negative.

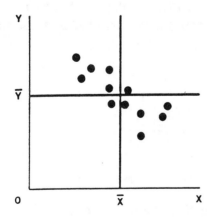

Fig 7.2(b): Negative relationship between X and Y

In Figure 7.2(c), if there is no obvious association between X and Y, the points will be scattered over all four quadrants and $\Sigma x_i y_i$ will tend to be small as the negative values largely balance out with the positive values.

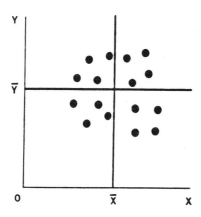

Fig 7.2(c):   No relationship between X and Y

7.3   THE PRODUCT MOMENT CORRELATION COEFFICIENT

The value $\Sigma x_i y_i$ is affected by the scale of measurement of X and Y and also by the number of observations.   An ideal measure is not affected by these factors.

Such a measure is

$$r = \frac{\Sigma x_i \, y_i}{\sqrt{(\Sigma x_i^2 \Sigma y_i^2)}}$$

where

x_i = the deviation of the X_i value from the mean X

y_i = the deviation of the Y_i value from the mean Y

r is called the **product moment coefficient of correlation** (sometimes called Pearson's coefficient of correlation).

The value of r varies between the extreme values of - 1 and + 1. **If r = - 1** there is perfect negative (or inverse) correlation and a straight line exactly fits the points. High values of Y go with low values of X, as in Figure 7.3.

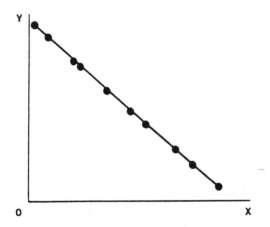

Fig 7.3: Perfect negative correlation (r = -1)

If r = 0 there is no correlation between X and Y. The points on the diagram would be scattered throughout the plane and no straight line could be said to properly represent the relationship between X and Y, as in Figure 7.4.

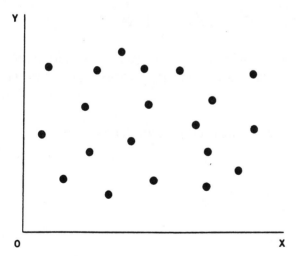

Fig 7.4: No correlation (r = 0)

If r = +1 there is perfect positive correlation. A straight line exactly fits the points. High values of X go with high values of Y, as in Figure 7.5.

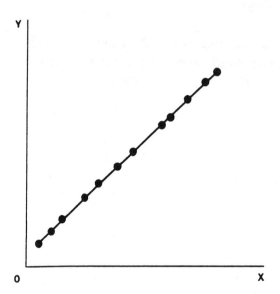

Fig 7.5: Perfect positive correlation (r = +1)

The closer the value of r to +1, the higher the degree of positive correlation. The closer the value of r to -1, the higher the degree of negative correlation. The closer the value of r to zero, the lower the degree of correlation.

The significance of the value of r is explained in section 7.8.

7.4   EXAMPLE OF POSITIVE CORRELATION

The figures in Table 7.1 relate the number of mortgage applications received by a building society for a particular category of property to an index of property prices for each year.

We wish to calculate the product moment correlation coefficient.

Table 7.1 Relation between mortgage applications and price index

Year	Number of Applications (00's) (X)	Price Index (Y)
1989	30	104
1990	37	128
1991	40	146
1992	42	170
1993	44	218
1994	53	230

$$\text{The mean of } X : \overline{X} = \frac{\Sigma X}{n} = \frac{246}{6} = 41$$

$$\text{The mean of } Y : \overline{Y} = \frac{\Sigma Y}{n} = \frac{996}{6} = 166$$

x = the deviation from $\overline{X}$ of each year's X value

y = the deviation from $\overline{Y}$ of each year's Y value

Therefore we have the values shown in Table 7.2.

Table 7.2: Calculation of product moment correlation coefficient between mortgage applications and price index

Year	x	y	x^2	y^2	xy
1989	-11	-62	121	3 844	682
1990	-4	-38	16	1 444	152
1991	-1	-20	1	400	20
1992	1	4	1	16	4
1993	3	52	9	2 704	156
1994	12	64	144	4 096	768
			292	12 504	1 782

For the correlation coefficient formula, we now have the values

$$\Sigma x^2 \quad = \quad 292$$

$$\Sigma y^2 \quad = \quad 12\ 504$$

$$\Sigma xy \quad = \quad 1\ 782$$

$$r = \frac{1\ 782}{\sqrt{(292 \times 12\ 504)}} = +0.933$$

This value for r indicates a fairly high degree of correlation between the two sets of values.

7.5   EXAMPLE OF NEGATIVE CORRELATION

Table 7.3 shows the index numbers of sales of aluminium and wooden window frames by a certain supplier over a twelve-year period (1986 = 100 in both cases).

We wish to find the degree of correlation between these two sets of figures.

Table 7.3: Index numbers of sales of window frames

Year	Index of Sales of Aluminium Frames (X)	Index of Sales of Wooden Frames (Y)
1983	91	116
1984	92	115
1985	91	113
1986	100	100
1987	112	96
1988	119	103
1989	128	96
1990	133	89
1991	139	91
1992	155	92
1993	163	90
1994	165	87
	1 488	1 188

Finding the means:

$$\overline{X} = \frac{\Sigma X}{n} = \frac{1\ 488}{12} = 124$$

$$\overline{Y} = \frac{\Sigma Y}{n} = \frac{1\ 188}{12} = 99$$

Table 7.4: Calculation of product moment correlation coefficient sales of aluminium and wooden window frames

Year	x	y	x^2	y^2	xy
1983	-33	17	1 089	289	-561
1984	-32	16	1 024	256	-512
1985	-33	14	1 089	196	-462
1986	-24	1	576	1	-24
1987	-12	-3	144	9	+36
1988	-5	4	25	16	-20
1989	4	-3	16	9	-12
1990	9	-10	81	100	-90
1991	15	-8	225	64	-120
1992	31	-7	961	49	-217
1993	39	-9	1 521	81	-351
1994	41	-12	1 681	144	-492
			8 432	1 214	-2 825

We can find the values for the correlation coefficient formula. This is shown in Table 7.4.

$$r = \frac{-2\ 825}{\sqrt{(8\ 432 \times 1\ 214)}} = -0.883$$

In this example the correlation is obviously negative and it is important that the negative sign is put in front of the coefficient to show this.

7.6   RANK CORRELATION

Sometimes it is necessary to know whether there is any association between two variables, without necessarily needing to know the extent of the association.

Such a measure can be more easily computed than the product moment coefficient.

7.7 SPEARMAN'S COEFFICIENT OF RANK CORRELATION

This measure is calculated from data which have been put into ranked descending or ascending order.

The measure denoted by r_s is found by the following formula:

$$r_s = 1 - \frac{6 \Sigma d^2}{n(n^2 - 1)}$$

where d = the difference between the X and Y rankings for any pair of values

n = the number of pairs of values

The values obtained for r_s can vary between 0 and 1.

Example 7.1:

The examination marks which ten students obtained in Surveying and Statistics are given in Table 7.5. We wish to find whether there seems to be any association between the two sets of marks.

Table 7.5: Examination marks of ten students

Student	Surveying	Statistics
A	53	67
B	68	59
C	58	68
D	42	58
E	50	40
F	92	85
G	41	57
H	94	69
I	23	46
J	29	23

If the students' marks are ranked in descending order then the difference in rankings between the two subjects can be measured as in Table 7.6.

Table 7.6: Difference in rankings of marks for two subjects

Student	Surveying (X)	Statistics (Y)	Rank of X	Rank of Y	d	d^2
A	53	67	5	4	1	1
B	68	59	3	5	-2	4
C	58	68	4	3	1	1
D	42	58	7	6	1	1
E	50	40	6	9	-3	9
F	92	85	2	1	1	1
G	41	57	8	7	1	1
H	94	69	1	2	-1	1
I	23	46	10	8	2	4
J	29	23	9	10	-1	1
						$\overline{24}$

$$n = 10$$
$$\Sigma d^2 = 24$$

and

$$r_s = 1 - \frac{6 \times 24}{10(100 - 1)} = 1 - \frac{144}{990} = 0.85$$

The main problem of calculation of the rank correlation coefficient arises when two or more values are ranked equally.

There are two ways to deal with this problem.

1. If two values are, say, ranked equal 2nd, then give them both a ranking of 2 and rank the next value as 4th.

2. Alternatively, the rankings could be shared. Eg in the above mentioned case the values ranked 2nd could be considered to be sharing 2nd and 3rd rankings and so could both be given an averaged ranking of (2 + 3)/2 = 2.5. As before, the next value would be ranked 4th. Whichever method is chosen, it is important that it is consistently pursued throughout the calculation.

7.8   THE INTERPRETATION OF THE VALUE OF r

Obviously the closer to unity (+1 or -1) is the value of the coefficient, the higher is the degree of correlation, and a value close to 0 indicates that little correlation exists.

The extreme values of 1 or 0 are unlikely to occur very often in practice though and in most examples we are usually concerned with interpreting the significance of values between perhaps 0.5 and 0.99.

The value of r is affected by the numbers of pairs of values for the two variables. For a small sample of items, the value of r obtained should be treated carefully. With a small number some degree of correlation may arise purely by chance.

For a larger sample, a test of significance for r involves the calculation of the standard error of r which is written as

$$\sigma_r = \frac{1}{\sqrt{(n-1)}}$$

If the calculated r is more than approximately twice (or 1.96 to be precise) this standard error then we can say at the 0.05 level of confidence that there is a significant correlation.

Perhaps the most common misuse of the correlation coefficient arises when it is used to imply a causal relationship between variables. This is not its purpose.   It does nothing more than show the strength of a linear relationship.

A correlation coefficient calculated for two variables may have a high value, but the correlation may be of a spurious nature ie. the two variables may not be causally related but may both be associated with some other outside factor.

7.9   THE   CORRELATION   COEFFICIENT   FORMULA: A MATHEMATICAL NOTE

The formula for the correlation coefficient was given in section 7.3 as

$$r = \frac{\Sigma x_i y_i}{\sqrt{(\Sigma x_i^2 \Sigma y_i^2)}}$$

as this is a form which is considered to be the simplest to understand and to utilise.

However, the formula may be rewritten as

$$r = \frac{n\Sigma X_i Y_i - (\Sigma X_i)(\Sigma Y_i)}{\sqrt{([n\Sigma X_i^2 - (\Sigma X_i)^2][n\Sigma Y_i^2 - (\Sigma Y_i)^2])}}$$

This form has the virtue that it is not necessary to find the mean values and the deviations from the means as the data in its original form is used.   This may make for easier calculation in some examples.

To show the equivalence of these two versions of the correlation coefficient:

We defined $x_i = X_i - \overline{X}$ and $y_i = Y_i - \overline{Y}$

$$\therefore \quad r = \frac{\Sigma x_i y_i}{\sqrt{(\Sigma x_i^2 \Sigma y_i^2)}}$$

$$= \frac{\Sigma (X_i - \overline{X})(Y_i - \overline{Y})}{\sqrt{(\Sigma (X^2 - \overline{X})^2 \Sigma (Y_i - \overline{Y})^2)}}$$

Consider

$$\Sigma (X_i - \overline{X})(Y_i - \overline{Y}) \; when \; expanded$$

$$= \Sigma (X_i Y_i - X_i \overline{Y} - \overline{X} Y_i + \overline{X}\,\overline{Y})$$

$$= \Sigma X_i Y_i - \overline{Y}\Sigma X_i - \overline{X}\Sigma Y_i + n\overline{X}\,\overline{Y}$$

$$= \Sigma X_i Y_i - \frac{\Sigma Y_i}{n}\Sigma X_i - \frac{\Sigma X_i}{n}\Sigma Y_i + n\frac{\Sigma X_i}{n}\frac{\Sigma Y_i}{n}$$

$$= \Sigma X_i Y_i - \frac{(\Sigma X_i)(\Sigma Y_i)}{n}$$

$$= \frac{n\Sigma X_i Y_i - (\Sigma X_i)(\Sigma Y_i)}{n}$$

In a similar fashion,

$$\Sigma (X_i - \overline{X})^2 = \frac{n\Sigma X_i^2 - (\Sigma X_i)^2}{n}$$

and

$$\Sigma (Y_i - \overline{Y})^2 = \frac{n\Sigma Y_i^2 - (\Sigma Y_i)^2}{n}$$

$$\therefore \quad r = \frac{\dfrac{n\Sigma X_i Y_i - (\Sigma X_i)(\Sigma Y_i)}{n}}{\sqrt{(\{[n\Sigma X_i^2 - (\Sigma X_i)^2]/n\}\{[n\Sigma Y_i^2 - (\Sigma Y_i)^2]/n\})}}$$

$$= \frac{n\Sigma X_i Y_i - (\Sigma X_i)(\Sigma Y_i)}{\sqrt{([n\Sigma X_i^2 - (\Sigma X_i)^2][n\Sigma Y_i^2 - (\Sigma Y_i)^2])}}$$

7.10 EXERCISES

1. The data contained in the table below can be used to assess the strength of the link between yields on short-term and long-term investments. Use the set of data in the table to demonstrate how the product moment correlation coefficient can be estimated. Indicate how these results could be improved.

Short and long-term yields

At Last Day of Month	Three Month Treasury Bill Yield (%)	2½% Consols Yield (%)
January	5.83	10.01
February	6.25	11.30
March	6.02	11.42
April	7.03	12.01
May	8.55	12.20
June	9.33	12.41
July	9.19	12.23
August	8.91	12.28
September	9.19	12.33
October	10.36	12.46
November	11.56	12.51
December	11.64	12.33

2. Use the data contained in the following table to estimate the level of linear association between the two factors. Comment on the adequacy of this statistical measure in this specific context.

	Average per cent Growth in Land Prices	Per cent Growth in Population
Wales	16.2	0.33
Northern	36.3	0.09
East Anglia	41.5	1.43
East Midlands	29.4	0.72
Yorkshire & Humberside	23.8	0.21
West Midlands	21.9	0.53
South West	34.0	1.08
North West	28.0	0.06
South East	30.7	0.38
England & Wales	30.0	0.32

8

TIME SERIES ANALYSIS

8.1   INTRODUCTION

A time series is the successive measurement of the size or value of a variable over time.

Example 8.1:

A typical example of how data vary over time is shown by example in Table 8.1, which shows the number of permanent dwellings started in Northern England for each quarter for a three year period.

Table 8.1: Permanent dwellings starts in each quarter
(Source: *Housing and Construction Statistics*)

Year 1	1st quarter	2 922
	2nd quarter	5 197
	3rd quarter	3 975
	4th quarter	3 203
Year 2	1st quarter	2 284
	2nd quarter	4 713
	3rd quarter	3 679
	4th quarter	3 082
Year 3	1st quarter	1 626
	2nd quarter	4 273
	3rd quarter	3 060
	4th quarter	3 380

Many sets of figures which vary over time have an element of **seasonal** or **cyclical** variation in their pattern e.g. house building statistics often show a marked variation between the summer and winter months, property sales statistics indicate that sales move more rapidly in periods of economic growth.

In many cases it may be useful to remove the variation element from a time series in order to estimate the **trend** for prediction purposes.

8.2 THE METHOD OF MOVING AVERAGES

We can deal with seasonal variations by the **method of moving averages**. From the actual time series data in the example, we are interested in removing the seasonal element (e.g. the fact that the number of housing starts is invariably higher in the second quarter than in the first quarter) in order to find the **trend**.

The steps we take to employ this method are as follows:

(a)   total the values four at a time, each time dropping one value and adding on the next one, and set the total against the second value;

(b)   add the four quarter totals, two at a time, to give the centred totals (centring is necessary whenever there is an even number of items in the moving average);

(c)   divide the values in the centred tables by 8 to find the **trend**. The reason for this is that each of the values in this centred table column is made up of eight values from the time series column.

If we take Example 8.1, the trend is found in Table 8.2. As can be seen from the resultant trend, the seasonal variations present in the original time series have now been removed. The values in the seasonally adjusted trend column show the downward movement in the series once the seasonal variation has been removed.

Table 8.2: Calculation of trend of housing starts

Year	Quarter	Housing starts	Total four quarters	Centred total	Trend
Year 1	I	2 922	-	-	-
	II	5 197	15 297	-	-
	III	3 975	14 659	29 956	3 744.5
	IV	3 203	14 175	28 834	3 604.25
Year 2	I	2 284	13 879	28 054	3 506.75
	II	4 713	13 758	27 637	3 454.625
	III	3 679	13 100	26 858	3 357.25
	IV	3 082	12 660	25 760	3 220.0
Year 3	I	1 625	12 041	24 701	3 087.625
	II	4 273	12 339	24 380	3 047.5
	II	3 060	-	-	-
	IV	3 380	-	-	-

One unfortunate feature of this method, however, is that the number of values in the trend column is inevitably less than the number in the original time series; values at the beginning and end of the series being 'chopped off'.

The original time series data and the trend line are shown in Figure 8.1. The smoothing effect of this method of moving averages is clearly shown.

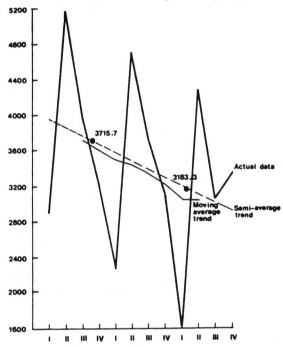

Fig 8.1: Original time series, moving average trend and semi-average trend: Example 8.1

8.3   CYCLICAL VARIATIONS

Due to the influence of booms and slumps in the economy, construction activity often follows a wave-like pattern over the years. In practice, this periodic cycle may last between five and fifteen years; this period being measured from one peak to the next. From a time series affected by this type of cycle the variation due to this element may again be removed by the method of moving averages.

Example 8.2:

Table 8.3 shows the turnover of a construction company for the previous fifteen years (year 15 is the most recent). From the figures the nature of cyclical pattern may not be immediately apparent. When the figures are plotted graphically, however, a five-year pattern can be perceived.

Table 8.3:   Turnover of a construction company

Year	Turnover (£m)
1	36
2	33
3	43
4	46
5	38
6	43
7	40
8	48
9	52
10	40
11	48
12	43
13	53
14	57
15	47

The cycle is twin peaked with a mini-boom in years 1, 6 and 11 and the major peak of the cycle also occurs at five-yearly intervals, i.e. years 4, 9 and 14.   In the construction industry this type of pattern is not uncommon.

To eliminate the cyclical variation from this series, the three five-year cycles can be identified, as too can the 1st period, 2nd period etc, of each cycle.   So, for instance, year 5 becomes 1st cycle, 5th period; year 6 becomes 2nd cycle, 1st period and so on.

A five-yearly moving average can then be calculated in order to arrive at the trend. This is carried out in Table 8.4.   The calculation of the trend in this case is simpler than in the previous example due to the fact that there is no need to draw up centred totals.   The totals of five values can be placed directly against the centre of the set of values i.e. the first five values sum to 196 and this figure is put against the middle of these five values (Year 3).

The values in the totals column can then be directly divided by 5 to give the trend figures.

The original time series and smoothed trend are shown in Fig 8.2.

Table 8.4: Calculation of five-yearly moving average

Year	Cycle	Period of Cycle	Turnover (£m)	Five-year Total	Trend
1	1st	1st	36	-	-
2		2nd	33	-	-
3		3rd	43	196	39.2
4		4th	46	203	40.6
5		5th	39	210	42.0
6	2nd	1st	43	215	43.0
7		2nd	40	221	44.2
8		3rd	48	223	44.6
9		4th	52	228	45.6
10		5th	40	231	46.2
11	3rd	1st	48	236	47.2
12		2nd	43	241	48.2
13		3rd	53	248	49.6
14		4th	57	-	-
15		5th	47	-	-

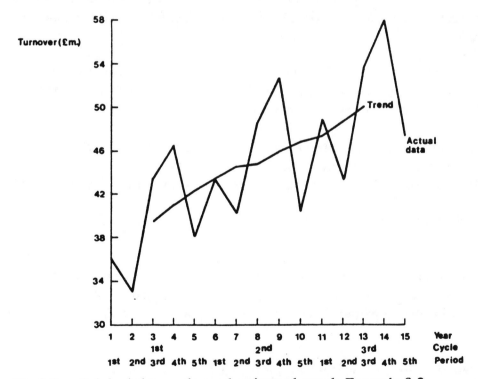

Fig 8.2: Original time series and estimated trend: Example 8.2

This method of moving averages can be used for any time series where a regular pattern exists. A three-year moving average may be appropriate in certain series. Certainly twelve-period moving averages are commonly encountered in the case of monthly statistics as are seven-period moving averages for daily produced data.

The major qualification to the use of the moving average method is that the trend inevitably covers a shorter period than the original time series and so a calculation involving a long moving average period must use a correspondingly large amount of data; enough to identify the regularity in the pattern.

8.4   THE USE OF TIME SERIES ANALYSIS

The main purpose of this type of analysis is to find out more about the behaviour of a time series by separating the various seasonal variations and/or cyclical variations from the trend. In forward planning, a knowledge of the trend contained in a series is vital and the identification of any pattern or regularity can greatly assist any prediction of future values in the series.

8.4.1 Extrapolation

In Example 8.2 the company in question may well be interested in estimating the turnover in years 16 and 17. To undertake such a calculation two factors would have to be considered.

The trend in the series. From the trend figures it can be seen that the trend rose from 39.2 to 49.6 between year 3 and year 13. This is a rise of 10.4 over the 10 years and thus constitutes an average increase of 1.04.

Using this average as the estimate of the annual increase in the trend, then three years after the last trend value (i.e. year 16), we can expect the trend to have risen to year 13's value + (3 × annual average increase) = 49.6 + (3 × 1.04) = 52.72.

In a similar fashion the estimate for the trend value for year 17 is 49.6 + (4 × 1.04) = 53.76.

The cyclical factor. Our estimate for a particular year must take account of the particular point in a cycle in which a year falls. In the designation of the five-year pattern year 16 is the 1st period of the 4th cycle and year 17 is the 2nd period of the 4th cycle.

The simplest way to take account of the cyclical factor is to find the average variation from the trend of all the 1st period years, 2nd period years etc. for which

108

we have the data and to adjust our predicted trend values by the appropriate average period of cycle variation. How this is done is shown in Tables 8.5 and 8.6.

Table 8.5: Calculation of variations from the trend

Cycle	Period	Turnover (£m)	Trend	Variation from Trend
1st	1st	36	-	
	2	33	-	
	3	43	39.2	+3.8
	4	46	40.6	+5.4
	5	38	42.0	4.0
2nd	1	43	43.0	0.0
	2	40	44.2	-4.2
	3	48	44.6	+3.4
	4	52	45.6	+6.4
	5	40	46.2	-6.2
3rd	1	48	47.2	+0.8
	2	43	48.2	-5.2
	3	53	49.6	+3.4
	4	57	-	-
	5	47	-	-

Table 8.6: Calculation of average variation for each year of the cycle

	lst Period	2nd Period	3rd Period	4th Period	5th Period
lst cycle	-	-	+3.8	+5.4	-4.0
2nd cycle	0.0	-4.2	+3.4	+6.4	-6.2
3rd cycle	+0.8	-5.2	+3.4	-	-
Total	+0.8	-9.4	+10.6	+11.8	-10.2
Average	+0.4	-4.7	+3.53	+5.9	-5.1

The figures in the variation from the trend column in Table 8.5 are found by subtracting the trend figure from the original time series figure for each year. So if the trend figure is less/more than the corresponding time series figure the variation has a positive/negative sign.

The variation figures are then set out in rows for each cycle as in Table 8.6 in order to find the average variation for each particular period of the cycle. (Note that the 3rd period's column total is the only one formed from three values because the first and last years in the trend column happen to fall at this point in the cycle. This column total must therefore be divided by three, unlike all the others which are divided by only two).

To return to the problem in hand, the trend figures we have found for years 16 and 17 must now be adjusted to allow for seasonal variations. Year 16's trend estimate of 52.72 needs to have +0.4 added to it as this is our estimate of the average 1st period of the cycle variation. This gives a total of 53.12. Year 17's trend estimate of 53.76 must similarly be adjusted by the average 2nd period variation of -4.7. This gives a total of 49.06.

Our final estimates, therefore, of the company's turnover in years 16 and 17 are £53.12m. and £49.06m respectively.

8.5 THE SEMI-AVERAGE METHOD

As the simplest form of trend is the straight line, one basic way of graphical estimation is to draw a straight line through the data to represent the trend. One method of doing this is the semi-average method.

This involves splitting the time series chronologically into halves and finding the arithmetic mean of the figures in each half. The mean value is then plotted against the centre in each half and these two points are then joined together.

As an example, the data on housing starts is split in this way in Table 8.7 and then the two means are found. The line formed by joining these points is shown in Figure 8.1, together with the estimated trend line from the moving average method and the actual data.

The acceptability of this simple method depends very much upon whether it seems reasonable to fit a straight line to the data.

Table 8.7: Calculation of semi-average for housing starts

2 922	3 679
5 197	3 082
3 975	1 626
3 203	4 273
2 284	3 060
4 713	3 380
$\frac{22\ 294}{6} = 3\ 715.7$	$\frac{19\ 100}{6} = 3\ 183.3$

8.6   TIME SERIES AND THE LEAST SQUARES METHOD

As we have see in Chapter 6, a useful way of fitting a straight line to two sets of data is the least squares method.

We can apply this method to time series data, when we can assume that the value of the variable is determined by the time period involved.

The two normal equations can be used to produce a linear equation $Y = a + bX$, where time is the independent variable, and where

a =   the value of the variable in period zero (i.e. normally the starting value in the series).

X =   the number of periods beyond this starting point.

Example 8.3:

The data in Table 8.8 show the mean value of all the contracts undertaken by a building organisation during a nine year period. We can find the equation of the trend line in the same manner as was used to find the regression line in earlier examples. However, due to the normally regular pattern (i.e. successive years in this example) of time series data, the procedure can be greatly simplified by changing the scale of the X's so that their sum is equal to zero.

111

Table 8.8: Mean value of contract undertaken by a building organisation

Year	1986	1987	1988	1989	1990	1991	1992	1993	1994
Value (£)	8 600	12 200	14 200	16 400	18 800	23 000	29 200	34 600	39 000

When this is done, the normal equations

$$\Sigma Y = na + b\Sigma X$$

and

$$\Sigma XY = a\Sigma X + b\Sigma X^2$$

become

$$\Sigma = na + (b \times 0)$$
$$\therefore \quad \Sigma Y = na$$

$$\therefore \quad a = \frac{\Sigma Y}{n}$$

and

$$\Sigma XY = (a \times 0) + b\Sigma X^2$$

$$\therefore \quad \Sigma XY = b\Sigma X^2$$

$$\therefore \quad b = \frac{\Sigma XY}{\Sigma X^2}$$

This simplification is achieved by setting the origin in the middle of the time periods. In the case of an odd number of periods the middle period becomes 0, so in this case we change the time scale to read:

1986	1987	1988	1989	1990	1991	1992	1993	1994
-4	-3	-2	-1	0	1	2	3	4

(Note that in the case of an even number of periods, the origin falls between the middle two).

The values necessary for a and b can now be found from Table 8.9.

112

Table 8.9: Change of time scale and calculation of a and b to find regression equation

	X	Y	X^2	XY
1986	-4	8 600	16	- 34 400
1987	-3	12 200	9	- 36 600
1988	-2	14 200	4	- 28 400
1989	-1	16 400	1	- 16 400
1990	0	18 800	0	0
1991	1	23 000	1	23 000
1992	2	29 200	4	58 400
1993	3	34 600	9	103 800
1994	4	39 000	16	156 000
	$\overline{0}$	196 000	$\overline{60}$	225 400

$\Sigma Y \quad = \quad 196\ 000, \ \Sigma X^2 \quad = \quad 60, \ \Sigma XY \quad = \quad 225\ 400, \ n = 9$

$a \quad = \dfrac{\Sigma Y}{n} \quad = \dfrac{196\ 000}{9} \quad = \ 21\ 777.8$

$b \quad = \dfrac{\Sigma XY}{\Sigma X^2} \quad = \dfrac{22\ 5400}{60} \quad = \ 3\ 756.6$

∴ The regression equation is

Y = 21 777.8 + 3 756.6 X

It must be made clear that this is the trend line which gives an estimated value of £21 777.8 for 1990 and not for 1986, the first year in the series.

This least squares trend line together with the moving average trend and actual data is shown in Figure 8.3.

The estimated value for 1986 is found by putting and X value of -4 into the regression equation i.e.

$\begin{aligned} Y \quad &= 21\ 777.8 + (3\ 756.6 \times - 4) \\ &= 21\ 777.8 - 15\ 026.4 \\ &= £6\ 751.2 \end{aligned}$

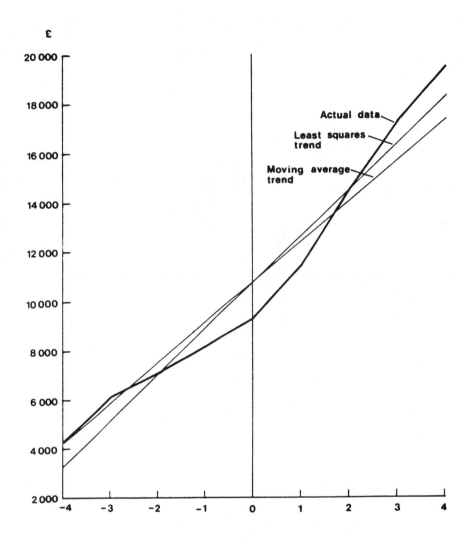

Fig 8.3: Original time series, moving average trend and least squares trend: Example 8.3

We can carry out extrapolation in the normal manner for the regression equation. So that if we want to estimate the value for 1995, for instance, we put in an X value of +5 into the equation i.e.

$$
\begin{aligned}
Y \quad &= \quad 21\ 777.8 + (3\ 756.6 \times 5) \\
&= \quad 21\ 777.8 + 18\ 783 \\
&= \quad £40\ 560.8
\end{aligned}
$$

114

8.7   EXERCISES

1.   Define a time series and give three examples of such a series. The following data give the construction index for a firm for a nine-year period.

Year	1986	1987	1988	1989	1990	1991	1992	1993	1994
Index	117	108	102	129	123	111	141	132	123

Examine the data and smooth the data using an appropriate moving average. Comment on the trends in the above data.

2.   Describe how you would calculate a four-point centred moving average. The following data give the amount of new projects started in £ million.

| Year | Quarter | | | |
	I	II	III	IV
1991	148 (-)	20 (-)	32 (62)	40 (65)
1992	164 (67)	28 (70)	40 (74)	56 (77)
1993	180 (79)	36 (81)	48 (-)	64 (-)

The second figure for each quarter is the four-point moving average. Calculate the average seasonal deviation for each quarter.

If the value for the first quarter of 1994 is 214 and, assuming that the seasonal variations are average, give an estimate for the three remaining quarters of 1994.

9

SAMPLING METHODS AND SAMPLING DISTRIBUTIONS

9.1   INTRODUCTION

Sampling from a population represents an attempt to assess some properties of a large number of items by a study of similar properties of a smaller group.   Sampling is useful in a number of situations.

1.   Where the whole of the population is not easily accessible, so that sampling is the only means available (e.g. taking sample bores on site to ascertain geological structure).

2.   Where a study of the whole population would be too expensive or take too long (e.g. collecting information on price changes from all retail outlets for a price index).

3.   Where the attribute being sampled would involve the destruction of the item (e.g. testing the breaking strength of building materials).

The usefulness of sampling depends upon two factors:

(a)   The sample must be chosen from the population in such a way that each member of the population has an equal chance of being chosen.   This is known as random **sampling**.

(b)   The size of the sample is also important.   Generally, the larger the sample the more reliance can be placed on the results being a cross-section of the population.

9.2   SAMPLING METHODS

Random sampling.   If a sample is chosen in a purely random manner, a representative selection can be obtained but this can be quite a difficult process.   It may be impossible to take a perfectly random sample in many cases but the avoidance of bias is extremely important.

The best method of random sampling is to use a table of random numbers.   Such a table is so called because there is no bias in the sequence of digits.   While the digits may be arranged as in Table 9.1, this has no significance. The table may be read up or down and the numbers used, one, two, three etc. at a time as required.

Table 9.1: Random numbers

7 2	9 5	1 4	0 4	8 4
9 7	4 2	7 2	3 6	0 8
8 0	2 1	0 1	4 9	6 2
1 5	5 7	3 5	0 3	4 6
6 7	2 4	6 3	7 1	3 4
8 0	1 6	9 5	6 3	6 8
1 7	9 1	5 9	9 5	3 2
7 9	3 5	1 3	8 4	6 7
0 6	8 1	2 7	0 5	2 9
0 8	3 4	2 8	9 0	5 8

Each digit is an independent sample taken from a population in which the digits 0, 1, ...9 are equally likely to occur.

Different methods of applying random sampling may be used, depending on the kind of population one wishes to survey. Such methods are considered below.

Stratified sampling. This approach can be used when there are obvious sub-groups within the population and it is desirable to make sure that each sub-group is suitably represented in the sample.

For instance, it may be known that 70 per cent of the private construction firms in a region are small firms (employing less than twenty workers), 20 per cent are medium sized (between twenty and 100 workers) and 10 per cent are large (over 100 workers). So if a sample of 200 firms were chosen for a survey and the sample were stratified according to size, the surveyed firms would be apportioned as follows: 140 small firms: 40 medium-sized firms: 20 large firms. This would be called a stratified sample. A fair representation is assured.

The attributes being surveyed can then be compared for the various groups.

Systematic sampling. This is a refinement of the basic method of simple random sampling. The method is to begin from a randomly selected item and then take every nth item (n being chosen to give the number required in the sample).

For example, there may be 500 houses on an estate and a sample survey of fifty houses may be required. One of the first ten houses could be chosen at random and then every tenth house thereafter.

Such a method is more convenient than ordinary random sampling and can be just as effective.

Multi-stage sampling. This method involves the reduction of a population to the required sample size by making choices from the population at various stages and the use of random sampling to make these choices at each stage.

If it were desired to interview 1 000 people at random from the various regions of England, ten counties could be chosen at random initially; within each county two districts could then be picked, and within each district a random sample of fifty people selected. This would give the total sample of 1 000.

The main advantage of this method is that the actual sampling procedure is likely to be made easier due to the greater concentration of the sample than would occur in a purely random sampling procedure from the total population.

The size of the sample. The larger the size of a sample, the more likely it is to give a representative picture of the population from which it has been chosen.

The accuracy of estimates of the characteristics of a population devised from sample information depends upon the size of the sample. As a general rule, the size of a sample should be at least thirty.

The problem in many sampling situations though, is that the larger the sample taken the greater the expense, time and effort involved and these factors have to be balanced against the extra accuracy which may result from taking a larger sample.

9.3 SAMPLING DISTRIBUTIONS

One main purpose of taking a sample from a population is to enable an estimate to be made of the mean of that population, on the basis of information from the sample. We are therefore interested in knowing what the probabilities are that a sample mean is likely to differ from the population mean by certain amounts.

If all the possible samples of size n were taken from a population and the mean of each sample taken, then a sampling distribution of these means could be formed.

The mean of such a distribution of the sample means is called $\mu_{\bar{x}}$ and the standard deviation of the sample means from the true population mean is called $\sigma_{\bar{x}}$ and is referred to as the standard error of the mean.

The larger the size of the samples taken, the smaller the difference between a sample mean and the population mean can be expected to be. So the standard error is therefore given by the formula:

$$\sigma_{\bar{x}} = \sigma/\sqrt{n}$$

where σ = the standard deviation of the population, which can be substituted by the standard deviation of the sample (s) if the sample is large enough i.e.

$$n \geq 30$$

Also if $n \geq 30$, the **Central Limit theorem** is applicable. This states that the theoretical sampling distribution of $\bar{x}$ can be approximated to the normal distribution regardless of the way in which the population is distributed.

Using this theorem, it is possible to calculate the probability of obtaining various values for $\bar{x}$ (the sample mean).

Example 9.1:

If the true mean height of all the students in a large college is 174.5cm and the standard error is 4.5cm, find the probability that a sample of 100 students will have a mean height of more than 175.2cm.

The mean of the sampling distribution is equal to the population mean (μ)

$$\mu_{\bar{x}} = \mu = 174.5$$

and the standard error of the sampling distribution is

$$\sigma_{\bar{x}} = \sigma/\sqrt{n} = \frac{4.5}{10} = 0.45$$

The standard normal distribution for x and the calculation of z values were explained in section 4.9. In a similar manner, the sampling distribution of $\bar{x}$, with mean $\mu_{\bar{x}}$ and standard error $\sigma_{\bar{x}}$ can also be standardised. We have:

$$z = \frac{\overline{X} - \mu_{\overline{X}}}{\sigma_{\overline{X}}}$$

Putting the appropriate values into the formula gives:

$$z = \frac{175.2 - 174.5}{0.45} = 1.56$$

We are interested in finding the area to the right of $z = 1.56$ as shown in Figure 9.1.

From the z table, the area to the left of $z = 1.56$ is 0.9406 and so the area we want is 1 - 0.9406 = 0.0594, which is the probability of the sample having a mean greater than 175.2cm.

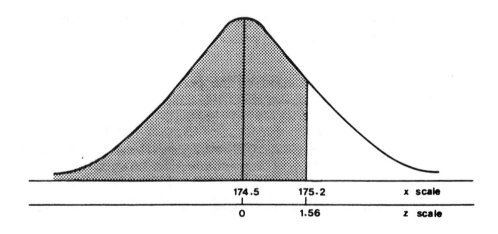

	174.5	175.2	x scale
	0	1.56	z scale

Fig 9.1: Conversion to the z scale

9.4 THE USE OF CONFIDENCE LIMITS IN THE ESTIMATION OF MEANS

If a single sample is taken and the sample mean found, then it is obviously impossible to determine the population mean precisely from such information. What we can do, though, is to establish limits within which the true population mean will fall, with a specified probability.

These limits are called confidence limits, and their determination is based upon our knowledge of the characteristics of the normal distribution.

As already shown in section 4.8, we know that 95 per cent of the area under a normal curve lies within two (or 1.96 to be exact) standard deviations of the mean value.

So, for the sampling distribution of means which has a mean μ_x and standard error of $\sigma/\sqrt{n}$ we can say that if $\bar{x}$ is the mean of a sample, then with a probability of 0.95 the standardised z value $(= (\bar{x} - \mu_{\bar{x}})/(\sigma/\sqrt{n}))$ will lie between - 1.96 and + 1.96.

This can be written as:

$$-1.96 \ \langle \ \frac{\bar{x} - \mu_{\bar{x}}}{\sigma/\sqrt{n}} \ \langle \ + 1.96$$

$$\therefore \ -1.96 \ \frac{\sigma}{\sqrt{n}} \ \langle \ \bar{x} - \mu_{\bar{x}} \ \langle \ + 1.96 \frac{\sigma}{\sqrt{n}}$$

$$\therefore \ \bar{x} - 1.96 \ \frac{\sigma}{\sqrt{n}} \ \langle \ \mu_{\bar{x}} \ \langle \ \bar{x} + 1.96 \ \frac{\sigma}{\sqrt{n}}$$

Thus with a probability of 0.95, i.e. 95 per cent confidence, we can claim that the interval $\bar{x}$ - 1.96 $(\sigma/\sqrt{n})$ to $\bar{x}$ + 1.96 $(\sigma/\sqrt{n})$ contains $\mu_{\bar{x}}$ $(=\mu)$.

This is therefore called the 95 per cent confidence interval.

As stated earlier, the mean of the sampling distribution is equal to the population mean and, for a large sample, σ is approximated by the sample standard deviation, s.

This means that the confidence interval can be rewritten as

$$\bar{x} - 1.96 \ \frac{s}{\sqrt{n}} \ \langle \ \mu \ \langle \ \bar{x} + 1.96 \ \frac{s}{\sqrt{n}}$$

Example 9.2:

A random sample of the weekly wages of 900 men employed in the construction industry in 1994 gave a mean weekly wage of £220 with a standard deviation of £19.50.

121

With 95 per cent confidence, find the limits within which the population mean weekly wage lies.

Here $\bar{x}$ = 220, s = 19.5 and n = 900. So the 95 per cent confidence interval is

$$220 - 1.96 \; \frac{19.5}{\sqrt{900}} \; \langle \; \mu \; \langle \; 220 + 1.96 \; \frac{19.5}{\sqrt{900}}$$

$$218.73 \; \langle \; \mu \; \langle \; 221.27$$

i.e. the 95 per cent confidence limits are £218.73 and £221.27.

It may well be the case that in certain situations it is necessary to find an interval within which our estimate of the population mean lies with a greater degree of confidence.

We can therefore further specify 98 per cent confidence limits as:

$$\bar{x} \pm 2.33 \; \frac{s}{\sqrt{n}}$$

and 99 per cent confidence limits as:

$$\bar{x} \pm 2.58 \; \frac{s}{\sqrt{n}}$$

Obviously in any particular estimation, the greater the degree of confidence the wider apart the limits must be.

When sample information is used as a basis for the estimation of the population mean then the confidence interval needs to be specified.

9.5 SIGNIFICANCE TESTS

Sometimes when sample information is used, or experiments are carried out, we may wish to find out whether the results obtained are within the range within which we expect them to be.

What often happens is that a hypothesis is put forward (the **null hypothesis**) and we wish to test whether there is consistency between the sample results and the hypothesis.

A test of significance can be used to 'test' the hypothesis. On the basis of sample information it is possible that we could reject the null hypothesis when the hypothesis is in fact a true one. We can specify the probability of such an error and call it the **level of significance** (depicted by α). We usually use $\alpha = 0.05$ or 0.01.

Example of a significance test. Suppose we want to test the hypothesis that the average value of a type of property in a certain area is £50 000 and we find that a random sample of 100 properties in the area had a mean value of £48 500 and a standard deviation of £7 200.

Our null hypothesis (H_o) can be stated as:

$$H_o : \mu = £50\ 000$$

and as the alternative is that the population mean value is not £50 000 we have an alternative hypothesis (H_1) of

$$H_1: \mu \neq £50\ 000$$

We specify a level of significance of 0.05. As we know that $z = (\bar{x} - \mu)/(s/\sqrt{n})$ has a standard normal distribution, we can reject the null hypothesis if z is outside the range -1.96 to + 1.96 (the critical values) but accept it if it is within that range, as shown in Fig. 9.2. This is called the decision rule. We have here

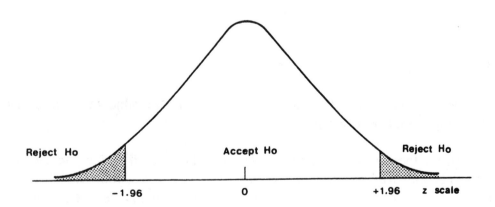

Fig 9.2: Two-tail significance test (0.05 level)

$$z = \frac{48\ 500 - 50\ 000}{7\ 200/\sqrt{100}} = -2.08$$

This means we reject the hypothesis that the population mean value is £50 000 at the 0.05 level of significance. Significance tests at the 0.01 level can also be carried out using critical values of ±2.575. Also 'one-tail' tests using a critical value of $+1.645$ (or -1.645) at the 0.05 level (as depicted in Fig 9.3) can be used instead of the normal 'two tail test' if we wish to stipulate an alternative hypothesis that the population mean is above (or below) a certain level.

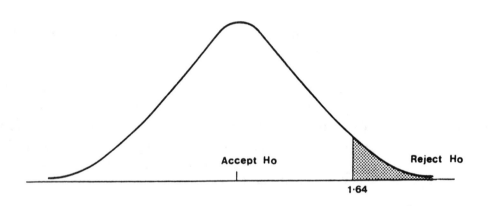

Fig 9.3:   One-tail significance test (0.05 level)

9.6   SMALL SAMPLES

If a sample of less than 30 is taken, then it is not possible to assume that the distribution of sample means is normal.

In this case, a theoretical sampling distribution called the **t distribution** can be used to enable confidence limits to be drawn up. This is also a symmetrical distribution, but the distribution depends upon the value (n - 1) where n is the size of the sample. The value (n - 1) is termed the number of degrees of freedom, and a table of t values differs from the z value table in that the corresponding areas vary according to the number of degrees of freedom.

For instance, we can calculate a 95 per cent confidence interval for μ as:

$$\overline{x} \pm t_{0.025} \frac{s}{\sqrt{n}}$$

As can be seen from Fig. 9.4, $t_{0.025}$ replaces 1.96 and has a value which varies according to the number of degrees of freedom. Reference to a set of t distribution tables which shows the $t_{0.025}$ etc. values with the appropriate number of degrees of freedom is required (see Table 2 in the Appendix).

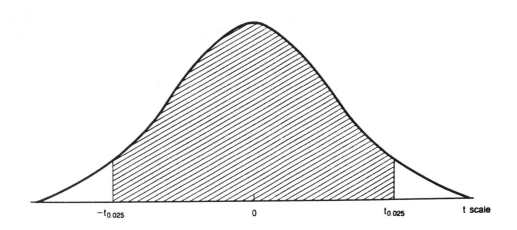

Fig 9.4: t- distribution with 95 per cent points

9.7 ESTIMATION OF PROPORTIONS

The purpose of sampling may not always be to yield information on the population mean but may be to estimate the proportion of a population which contains a certain attribute.

If the proportion of a sample which has a certain property is found, then confidence limits can be found for the true proportion of the population (π).

Where   p = the proportion of the sample found to possess the attribute
             q = the proportion not possessing the attribute
and   n = the size of sample

then a 95 per cent confidence interval for π is given by

$$\pi \pm 1.96 \sqrt{\frac{pq}{n}}$$

i.e. $\sqrt{(pq/n)}$ is the standard error.

Example 9.3:

A random sample of 800 houses in a town showed that 480 of the dwellings had a central heating system. Estimate the proportion of houses in the whole town with central heating.

The 95 per cent confidence limits are therefore:

$$0.6 \pm 1.96 \sqrt{\left(\frac{0.6 \times 0.4}{800}\right)} = 0.6 \pm 0.0339$$

i.e. the population proportion is estimated to be between 0.5661 and 0.6339.

9.8   EXERCISES

1.   Explain and illustrate the principles of simple random sampling and of stratified random sampling used in the collection of economic and financial data. Identify the relative advantages and disadvantages of the two methods.

2.   Statistics has been defined as the science of drawing valid conclusions about populations from samples.

   (a)   Describe the principal methods of sampling, discussing their particular uses and limitations.

   (b)   An estate agent wishes to estimate the typical cost of accommodation in his town. He takes a sample of eight-one houses from his recent circulars. The prices of these houses show an arithmetic mean of £66 330 and a standard deviation of £13 000.

   On the assumption that the data represent a valid sample and this mean is also appropriate, estimate the limits of the population mean with 95 per cent confidence.

   (c)   What other reservations should we place on the assumption that £66 330 is a fair estimate of the cost of accommodation in his town?

10

INFERENCE AND SIGNIFICANCE TESTING: FURTHER TECHNIQUES

10.1 INTRODUCTION

We have seen that the normal distribution can be used to test hypotheses by enabling us to estimate how frequently a given result would be likely to arise on a purely random basis from an assumed population. If it is quite likely, then we attach no significance to the result. The parameters used in this test are the mean and the standard deviation.

Other parameters can be obtained which are of particular importance where the normal curve does not apply. Of these the **chi-squared** test is perhaps the most important.   It is used to test the significance of the differences between the frequencies of an actual observed distribution and the frequencies to be expected if the distribution obeyed strictly some stated law.

10.2 THE CHI-SQUARED TEST

The Greek letter X in its squared form is used (chi, pronounced ky), defined so that

$$\chi^2 \ = \ \sum \frac{(f_A - f_E)^2}{f_E}$$

where f_A represents the actual frequency of each item and f_E its expected frequency. Sometimes it is easier to use the equivalent form

$$\chi^2 \ = \ \sum \left(\frac{f_A^2}{f_E} \right) - N$$

which just involves squaring each actual frequency and dividing by its expected equivalent, summing the results and deducting, from the total, the total of the frequencies ($= N$).

The test can be used as an indication of the goodness of fit of some theoretical distribution to actual data. The theoretical distribution may be in the form of a curve the equation of which is known, or, more simply, could be the expected distribution of frequencies in the cells of a contingency table.

Table 10.1:   Comparison of actual (observed) and expected frequencies

(X)	Frequencies		$(f_A - f_E)$	$(f_A - f_E)^2$	$(f_A - f_E)^2/f_E$
	Actual (f_A) (Y)	Expected (f_E)			
1	18	22	-4	16	0.7273
2	36	34	-2	4	0.1176
3	50	48	2	4	0.0833
4	66	64	2	4	0.0625
5	81	82	-1	1	0.0122
6	105	102	3	9	0.0882
7	114	124	-10	100	0.8065
8	144	148	-4	16	0.1081
9	179	174	5	25	0.1437
10	207	202			0.1238
	1 000	1 000			2.2732

Table 10.1 shows a typical calculation of the first type. Actual or observed values of Y are shown for given values of X, and the expected frequencies have been calculated from the equation $Y = 12 + 9X + X^2$, which we may assume is the law being tested.

The calculated value of χ^2 is seen to be 2.27 and we have to use tables of χ^2 (see Appendix - Table 3) to find the probability of this value arriving from chance for the degrees of freedom associated with the data being tested. The number of degrees of freedom here is 10 - 1 = 9. If we work at the $\alpha = 0.05$ level of significance, the value of χ^2 would have to be greater than 16.9. Thus we conclude that the difference between the actual and the expected values is not significant. In other words, the actual distribution is a good approximation to the theoretical distribution.

10.3 CONTINGENCY TABLES

The term *contingency table* is applied to a table of *frequencies* where there is more than one column and more than one row. It is usual to refer to an (r x c) table to denote one having r rows and c columns. The rows are always denoted first.

We are often concerned with testing whether the distribution of observed frequencies in the various cells of the table accords with the expected distribution arrived at by applying some hypothesis.

Example: Suppose that we are intereted in the pass rates of construction students at different universities. The upper half of Table 10.2 shows the actual distribution of passes and failures of the construction students of three universities. We wish to test whether there is a significant difference between the universities with regard to their rates of success.

If there is no difference between the universities in this respect we should expect those who pass to be present in the same proportion in each of the columns. This proportion can be taken as that of the combined population, shown in the *total* column. Out of the total of 150 students, 120 pass, which is 80%. Applying this percentage to the totals of each university individually we have 80% of 40, 80% of 50, and 80% of 60. These are the expected passes which are entered in the lower table. The other expected figures can be filled in to make up the required totals.

In fact, with a (2 x 3) table we require only two of the six cells to be filled in to enable us to complete the rest, assuming the totals are given. A (2 x 3) table has, thus, only two degrees of freedom.

Table 10.2: Analysis of the performance of students of three universities in selected examinations

a. Actual

| | University | | | |
	A	B	C	Total
Pass	28	37	55	120
Fail	12	13	55	30
	40	50	60	150

130

b.   Expected, if there is no difference between the universities.

	University			Total
	A	B	C	
Pass	32	40	48	120
Fail	8	10	12	30
	40	50	60	150

A simple trial will show that, for any (r x c) table the number of degrees of freedom is (r - 1) (c - 1).

The chi-squared test can be applied directly to the contingency table, comparing the actual and expected frequencies.

For the Table 10.2 we have

$$\chi^2 = \frac{(28-32)^2}{32} + \frac{(37-40)^2}{40} + \frac{(55-48)^2}{48} + \frac{(12-8)^2}{8} \frac{(13-10)^2}{10} + \frac{(5-12)^2}{12} = 8.729.$$

The number of degrees of freedom is (2 - 1) (3 - 1) = 2.

So if we use α = .05, we will reject the null hypothesis that the two classifications (by university and by examination success) are independent if χ^2 > 5.99.

Since the value of the test statistic is χ^2 = 8.729, and this exceeds the critical value of χ^2 we reject the null hypothesis.

The data present sufficient evidence to indicate that the proportion of students passing their examinations varies amongst the universities.

10.4   ANALYSIS OF VARIANCE

We have already seen in this chapter that the chi-square test can be used to examine the difference between sample proportions and to make inferences about whether such samples are drawn from populations each having the same proportion. In this section, we will consider a technique known as **analysis of variance** (often abbreviated to ANOVA), which enables us to test for the significance of the difference between more than two sample means.

131

Using analysis of variance, we will be able to make inferences about whether our samples are drawn from populations having the same mean.

Analysis of variance will be useful in such situations as, say, comparing expenditure on housing by families in different areas of the country or testing which of four different training methods provides the largest improvement in operatives' productivity.

Example:

The data in Table 10.3 relate to average weekly expenditure on housing for five families in each of four different areas of the country.

Table 10.3: Average weekly expenditure on housing

Area A	Area B	Area C	Area D
32	56	40	37
35	47	36	38
30	44	44	45
28	55	33	44
25	48	47	36

The concern is to discover whether there appears to be any difference in expenditure in the four areas.

Our reason for using analysis of variance is to decide whether these four samples were drawn from populations with the same means. A formal statement of the null and alternative hypotheses we wish to test would be:

$$H_0 \quad : \quad \mu_A = \mu_B = \mu_C = \mu_D$$

$$H_1 \quad : \quad \mu_A, \mu_B, \mu_C \text{ and } \mu_D \text{ are } not \text{ all equal.}$$

Average expenditure for each area (i.e. x_A, etc.) may differ because of (a) area differences or (b) chance.

If the null hypothesis is true, the variation is due to (b) only.

If the null hypothesis is false, the variation is due to (a) and (b).

We compare the actual variation when null is true with the actual variation.

For our data, we can calculate the mean expenditure for each area and also the variance for each area (s^2_A etc. is calculated with n - 1 as the denominator).

$$\overline{X}_A = 30, \qquad \overline{X}_B = 50, \qquad \overline{X}_C = 40, \qquad \overline{X}_D = 40$$

$$s^2_A = 14.5, \qquad s_A^2 = 27.5, \qquad s_B^2 = 32.5, \qquad s_D^2 = 17.5$$

The measure of the actual variation is:

$$S^2_{\overline{x}_i} = \frac{\Sigma(\overline{x}_i - \overline{\overline{x}})^2}{k-1}$$

where $\overline{\overline{x}}$ is the overall mean of the total data and k is the number of sample means.

$$S^2_{\overline{x}_i} = \frac{(30-40)^2 + (50-40)^2 + (40-40)^2 + (40-40)^2}{3} = \frac{200}{3}$$

An assumption is that all the populations are normally distributed and have a common variance (σ^2).

If null is true, all four samples are drawn from normal populations with the same mean μ and same variance σ^2.

Therefore, we expect the $\overline{x}$'s to have a variance of σ^2/n (where n = the size of the sample).

σ^2 is unknown and we estimate it by:

$$S^2 = \frac{s_A^2 + s_B^2 + s_C^2 + s_D^2}{k}$$

$$= \frac{14.5 + 27.5 + 32.5 + 17.5}{4} = 23$$

Our estimate of the expected variance of $\bar{x}_i$ when null is true is:

$$\frac{S^2}{n} = \frac{23}{5}$$

We reject null if

$$S^2_{\bar{x}_i}$$

is sufficiently greater than S^2/n,

i.e. if

$$\frac{S^2_{\bar{x}_i}}{S^2/n} \quad \textit{is sufficiently} > 1$$

If null is true,

$$\frac{S^2_{\bar{x}_i}}{S^2/n} \quad \textit{has an F distribution}$$

with $[k - 1, k(n - 1)]$ degrees of freedom.

The number of degrees of freedom are $(3, 16)$ in this case, and from the F distribution table (Table 4 in the Appendix), with a level of significance of 0.05, the critical value for $F_{0.05}$ is 3.24.

We reject the null hypothesis if the test statistic is > 3.24.

For our data

$$\frac{S^2_{\bar{x}_i}}{S^2/n} = \frac{200/3}{23/5} = 14.5$$

We therefore reject the null hypothesis at the 0.05 level of significance, i.e. evidence suggests that area affects housing expenditure.

10.4 EXERCISES

1. During a given period, the production manager in a factory manufacturing building components recorded the number of hours for which each of its six machines were out of action due to mechanical breakdown. The observed results are given in the table. Do these data present sufficient evidence to indicate that some machines were worse than others in terms of time loss? (Handy hint: Use the mean number of hours as the expected value for each machine.) (Test at the $\alpha = 0.05$ level)

Machine Number	1	2	3	4	5	6
Hours	84	110	146	152	61	47

2. A survey of marketing managers in four different industries provided the data in the following tables, which give the managers' perceived attitudes towards market research.

    Do these data present sufficient evidence to indicate that the perceived value of market research differs among marketing managers in the four industries?

Perceived Value of Market Research	Industry Type			
	Insurance	Manufacturing	Construction	Retailing
Little Value	9	22	13	9
Moderate Value	29	41	6	17
Great Value	26	28	6	27
Total	64	91	25	53

3.   To test the effectiveness of four different preventive measures against the corrosion of cables, random samples of four pieces of cable for each of the four measures were taken, and the corrosion measured by the depths of the maximum pits.

Test at the 0.05 level of significance, whether the observed difference between the means obtained for the four measures can be attributed to chance.

Data are as follows:

Measure A	Measure B	Measure C	Measure D
4	7	5	11
6	13	4	10
4	10	4	9
10	14	7	14

————————————————————— **11** —————————————————————

NON-PARAMETRIC METHODS

11.1 INTRODUCTION

Most of the work in this book has been directed to interpretation and to testing the significance of statistics.

There are broadly two approaches:

(a)   Assume that the population from which the data are drawn is distributed in some established way, e.g. normally distributed.

(b)   Make no assumptions about the nature of the population but rely on the observations themselves, which must be random and independent.

The second approach gives rise to **non-parametric** or distribution-free methods, which are often quicker to apply and regarded as short-cut methods. Generally, where measures are involved (means etc.), the first or parametric approach is desirable. When the data are in the form of ranks or of counts (rank differences etc.), the non-parametric techniques may be more appropriate. We can sometimes switch from parametric to non-parametric methods by simplifying the data, e.g. representing it by a rank rather than by a measure. This usually involves discarding some of the information so that the test may be less precise.

The non-parametric methods that are presented in this chapter were chosen to solve a few of the same types of problems solved earlier by parametric methods. All of them are concerned with testing some hypothesis.

11.2 THE RANK-SUM TEST

One of the most useful tests in real-life situations is that of testing whether the means of two populations may be assumed to be equal. Such a test is often required when it is necessary to determine whether a new process or procedure is superior to an existing or standard one. If the sample sizes are small and the normality assumption required for the t-test is not justified, then a non-parametric test is needed. One such test that is designed to solve this problem is called the **rank sum test**.

As its name implies, it is based on using the ranks of measurements instead of the measurements themselves. The theory of the test means that we can test the

137

hypothesis that two population means are equal (H_0: $\mu_1 = \mu_2$) and the two variables have the same distribution, even though it is unknown.

Example:

Consider the following data which shows the output (in terms of number of tasks completed over a period of time) of two unequal groups of building craftsmen. The first group (Group A) are working under conditions of a productivity bonus scheme, whereas those in the second group (Group B) are not.

Group A	72, 58, 48, 94, 76, 44, 88, 42, 28, 22, 54, 36, 66
Group B	56, 82, 62, 24, 46, 74, 96, 90, 32, 50

The first step is to combine the two sets of figures and to arrange them in order of increasing size, as follows:

$$22, \underline{24}, 28, \underline{32}, 36, 42, 44, \underline{46}, 48, \underline{50}, 54, \underline{56},$$
$$58, \underline{62}, 66, 72, \underline{74}, 76, \underline{82}, 88, \underline{90}, 94, \underline{96}$$

(The entries for Group B are underlined)

These values are then replaced by their ranks to give:

$$1, \ \underline{2}, \ 3, \ \underline{4}, \ 5, \ 6, \ 7, \ \underline{8}, \ 9, \ \underline{10}, \ 11, \ \underline{12},$$
$$13, \ \underline{14}, \ 15, \ 16, \ \underline{17}, \ 18, \ \underline{19}, \ 20, \ \underline{21}, \ 22, \ \underline{23}$$

The ranks of the smaller set (Group B) are then summed. If this sum is denoted by R, then R = 130.

The distribution of R depends upon the size of the two samples, which are denoted by n_1 and n_2 (with n_1 denoting the smaller of the two samples).

As $n_2 > 10$, the distribution of R can be approximated by the normal distribution, with mean and standard deviation given by the formulae:

$$\mu_R = \frac{n_1(n_1 + n_2 + 1)}{2}$$

and

$$\sigma_R = \sqrt{(n_1 \, n_2)(n_1 + n_2 + 1) \, / 12}$$

Here $n_1 = 10$ and $n_2 = 13$, so:

$$\mu_R = 120$$

$$\text{and } \sigma_R = \sqrt{260} = 16.1$$

Under the assumption of an approximate normal distribution for R, the standard normal variable value for this problem is

$$Z = \frac{R - \mu_R}{\sigma_R} = \frac{130 - 120}{16.1} = 0.62$$

Since a two-sided test is being used here, and the critical regions for $\alpha = .05$ are those given by $z > 1.96$ and $z < -1.96$, the hypothesis $H_0 : \mu_1 = \mu_2$ is accepted.

As stated earlier, this test is actually a test of the hypothesis that the two samples have the same distribution. It is therefore conceivable that the two distributions might have the same means but have sufficiently different other characteristics to produce significant sample differences in testing. That possibility, however, seldom occurs in real-life situations.

11.3   THE SIGN TEST FOR MATCHED PAIRS

Some of the simplest of the non-parametric methods involve **sign tests**. Suppose that we wish to compare consumer ratings (on a scale of 1 to 10 in which 10 is 'best') of two new house designs (A and B). Six housebuyers are randomly selected from the consumer group and each one rates the two designs. The results are shown in Table 11.1.

Table 11.1: Ratings for house designs

| Consumer | House Design | | + / - |
	A	B	
1	10	6	+
2	7	5	+
3	7	9	-
4	5	2	+
5	6	7	-
6	9	6	+

The question we want to answer is:

> Do the data present sufficient evidence to indicate a difference in consumer preference for the two designs?

No complicated statistical test is needed to answer the question. We can use a rough-and-ready non-parametric test procedure known as the sign test.

The ratings are compared by placing a '+' or '-' sign in the adjacent column in the table, depending upon whether the first of the pair is greater or smaller.

Assuming no differences arise through chance, there will be n/2 (= 6/2 = 3) which are plus and n/2 which are minus, in the long-run of sampling. We may say that the probability (p) of '+' is 0.5 and the probability (q) of minus is also 0.5.

The significance of any actual number of '+' values may be tested as an attribute, using the fact that the standard error is $\sqrt{npq}$, and that 1.96 times this, is at the 5% level of significance.

In our example, the standard error should be:

$$\sqrt{(6 \times 0.5 \times 0.5)} \quad = \quad 1.224$$

At the 5% confidence level, we are concerned with deviations of more than 1.96 x 1.224 = 2.4.

We should expect 95% of samples to be in the range 3 $\pm$ 2.4, i.e. 0.6 to 5.4.

As the rating for design A exceeds that for design B for four of the consumers, we are not justified in saying that the preferences for the designs do differ significantly at this level.

11.4 THE WILCOXON TEST FOR MATCHED PAIRS

The sign test is a very simple test to apply when the data come in the form of matched pairs, but its very simplicity suggests that a non-parametric test that uses the values of the variables, rather than just the signs of their differences, should produce a more efficient test.

A test of this type, called the **Wilcoxon signed rank test** uses both the signs of the paired differences and also their rank sums.

Example:

The procedure that is used in applying this test can be illustrated on the house design ratings problem using the data in Table 11.1.

First, calculate the differences of all the sample pairs and then ignore the signs of these differences and rank them according to these absolute values. The results of these steps are shown in Table 11.2.

Table 11.2: Data for Wilcoxon Test

Difference	Rank
4	6
2	2.5
-2	2.5
3	4.5
-1	1
3	4.5

The final step in preparing for the test is to sum the ranks of the positive differences. If this sum is denoted by V, then here V = 17.5.

Although it is possible to derive a distribution for the variable V, under the hypothesis that the two samples come from identical populations, it usually suffices to use the approximate normal distribution that has been found for this variable, under this hypothesis. Its mean and standard deviation are given by the formulae:

$$\mu_v = \frac{n(n + 1)}{4}$$

and

$$\sigma_v = \sqrt{n(n + 1)(2n + 1)/24}$$

The value of 'n' here is the total number of non-zero differences. In this problem, there are no zero differences, so n = 6, and

$$\mu_v = 10.5 \quad \text{and} \quad \sigma_v = 4.77$$

Hence,

$$Z = \frac{V - \mu_v}{\sigma_v} = \frac{17.5 - 10.5}{4.77} = 1.47$$

At the .05 level the critical region is z > 1.96, so, again we may conclude that preferences for the designs do not appear to differ significantly.

The preceding non-parametric methods are just a few of the many such methods available.

Empirical investigations have shown that many of the parametric tests that require a normality assumption may be good even when the basic variable has a distribution quite different from that of a normal variable; therefore, one should hesitate to discard a parametric test in favour of a non-parametric one, unless the normality assumption is seriously violated, or unless there exists a non-parametric test that is almost as good as the parametric test for solving the problem.

11.5 EXERCISES

1. Two companies manufacture precast concrete beams and the only difference between the two companies' products is that Company X uses a certain additive in the mix whereas Company Y does not.

    Breakage tests were carried out on 15 of Company X's beams and 12 of Company Y's with the following results:

Company X	2 091	2 285	2 023	2 705	2 595	2 455
	2 455	2 659	2 205	2 932	2 659	2 545
	2 120	2 640	2 375			
Company Y	2 341	2 636	2 227	2 750	2 523	2 614
	2 068	2 250	2 841	2 591	2 432	2 409

Using a rank-sum test, indicate whether these data provide sufficient evidence that the breaking strength differs for the two sets of beams (Use $\alpha = .05$).

2. The following table shows the examination scores of twelve matched pairs of construction students, in which a half of them were taught by Method A and a half by Method B.

Method A	65	40	63	78	67	34	76	57	75	88	77	75
Method B	60	42	65	71	62	35	74	54	71	82	78	67

Use the sign test to test the hypothesis that the means of the two groups are equal.

143

ANSWERS TO SELECTED EXERCISES

Chapter 2:

Ex. 1 -   Arithmetic mean = 4.85m^2
Median (by calculation) = 4.844m^2
Mode (by calculation) = 4.833m^2

Chapter 3:

Ex. 1 -   Building technology.   Mean = 54.5 marks
Standard deviation = 18 marks
Construction.   Mean = 54.875 marks
Standard deviation = 13.54 marks

Ex. 2 -   Median = £62 999.5
Quartile deviation = £4 142.6

Ex. 3 -   Arithmetic mean = 9.62 km
Standard deviation = 3.57 km

Chapter 4:

Ex. 1 -   (a) 0.0005   (b) 0.0440
(c) 0.0006   (d) 0.9506

Ex. 2 -   (a) P (machine 2 idle) = 0.1
P (machine 3 working) = 0.5
(b) 0.210   (c) 0.648   (d) 0.166

Chapter 5:

Ex. 1 -   (b) (i)   If an aggregative base weighted price index is compiled using 1992 as base year and taking 1992 quantities as weights, the index series is:
1992   100
1993   116.4
1994   149.1

(b) (ii)   If an aggregative base weighted quantity index is compiled using 1992 as base year and taking 1992 prices as weights, the index series is:

1992	100
1993	113.6
1994	138.2

Ex. 2 -   Using 1990 prices as weights, the index series is:

1990	100
1991	118.3
1992	139.1
1993	169.6

Ex. 3 -   (c)

1991	100
1992	120.1
1993	143.3

Chapter 6:

Ex. 2 - $Y = 4.2985 + 0.0619 X$

(i) £14.79

(ii) £20.98

Chapter 7:

Ex. 1 - $r = + 0.790$

$r = + 0.919$

Chapter 8:

Ex. 1 -   Using a three year moving average, the trend is calculated as:

1987	109
1988	113
1989	118
1990	121
1991	125
1992	128
1993	132

Ex. 2 - The average seasonal variations are:

Quarter	I	II	III	IV
(£m)	+99	-43.5	-32	-23

The estimates for the last three quarters of 1994 are:

Quarter	I	III	IV
(£m)	57(.6875)	72(.75)	85(.3125)

(These estimates are based on the addition of the 1994 (I) value to the time series)

Chapter 9:

Ex. 3 - (b) 95% confidence limits: £63 498.9 to £69 161.1

Chapter 10:

Ex. 1 - Yes; $X^2 = 95.06$ $(X^2_{.05} = 11.07)$

Ex. 2 - Yes; $X^2 = 20.91$ $(X^2_{.05} = 12.59)$

Ex. 3 - $F = 6.65$ $(F_{.05} = 3.49)$
Observed difference cannot be attributed to chance.

Chapter 11:

Ex. 2 - At the .05 level, we would expect 95% of samples to be in the range 6 ± 3.395 (ie. 2.605 to 9.395). The marks of eight students under Method A are higher. We are unable to reject the hypothesis that the means of the two groups are equal.

APPENDIX

Table 1: The Normal Distribution Function

Z	Area	Z	Area	Z	Area	Z	Area
0.00	0.5000	0.30	0.6179	0.60	0.7257	0.90	0.8159
0.01	0.5040	0.31	0.6217	0.61	0.7291	0.91	0.8186
0.02	0.5080	0.32	0.6255	0.62	0.7324	0.92	0.8212
0.03	0.5120	0.33	0.6293	0.63	0.7357	0.93	0.8238
0.04	0.5160	0.34	0.6331	0.64	0.7389	0.94	0.8264
0.05	0.5199	0.35	0.6368	0.65	0.7422	0.95	0.8289
0.06	0.5239	0.36	0.6406	0.66	0.7454	0.96	0.8315
0.07	0.5279	0.37	0.6443	0.67	0.7486	0.97	0.8340
0.08	0.5319	0.38	0.6480	0.67	0.7517	0.89	0.8365
0.09	0.5359	0.39	0.6517	0.69	0.7549	0.99	0.8389
0.10	0.5398	0.40	0.6554	0.70	0.7580	1.00	0.8413
0.11	0.5438	0.41	0.6591	0.71	0.7611	1.01	0.8438
0.12	0.5478	0.42	0.6628	0.72	0.7642	1.02	0.8461
0.13	0.5517	0.43	0.6664	0.73	0.7673	1.03	0.8485
0.14	0.5557	0.44	0.6700	0.74	0.7704	1.04	0.8508
0.15	0.5596	0.45	0.6736	0.75	0.7734	1.05	0.8531
0.16	0.5636	0.46	0.6772	0.76	0.7764	1.06	0.8554
0.17	0.5675	0.47	0.6808	0.77	0.7794	1.07	0.8577
0.18	0.5714	0.48	0.6844	0.78	0.7823	1.08	0.8599
0.19	0.5753	0.49	0.6879	0.79	0.7852	1.09	0.8621
0.20	0.5793	0.50	0.6915	0.80	0.7881	1.10	0.8643
0.21	0.5832	0.51	0.6950	0.81	0.7910	1.11	0.8665
0.22	0.5871	0.52	0.6985	0.82	0.7939	1.12	0.8686
0.23	0.5910	0.53	0.7019	0.83	0.7967	1.13	0.8708
0.24	0.5948	0.54	0.7054	0.84	0.7995	1.14	0.8729
0.25	0.5987	0.55	0.7088	0.85	0.8023	1.15	0.8749
0.26	0.6026	0.56	0.7123	0.86	0.8051	1.16	0.8770
0.27	0.6064	0.57	0.7157	0.87	0.8078	1.17	0.8790
0.28	0.6103	0.58	0.7190	0.88	0.8106	1.18	0.8810
0.29	0.6141	0.59	0.7224	0.89	0.8133	1.19	0.8830

Table 1: The Normal Distribution Function / continued ...

Z	Area	Z	Area	Z	Area	Z	Area
1.20	0.8849	1.50	0.9332	1.80	0.9641	2.05	0.97982
1.21	0.8869	1.51	0.9345	1.81	0.9649	2.06	0.98030
1.22	0.8888	1.52	0.9357	1.82	0.9656	2.07	0.98077
1.23	0.8907	1.53	0.9370	1.83	0.9664	2.08	0.98124
1.24	0.8925	1.54	0.9382	1.84	0.9671	2.09	0.98169
1.25	0.8944	1.55	0.9394	1.85	0.9678	2.10	0.98214
1.26	0.8962	1.56	0.9406	1.86	0.9686	2.11	0.98257
1.27	0.8980	1.57	0.9418	1.87	0.9693	2.12	0.98300
1.28	0.8997	1.58	0.9429	1.88	0.9699	2.13	0.98341
1.29	0.9015	1.59	0.9441	1.89	0.9671	2.14	0.98382
1.30	0.9032	1.60	0.9452	1.85	0.9678	2.15	0.98422
1.31	0.9049	1.61	0.9463	1.86	0.9686	2.16	0.98461
1.32	0.9066	1.62	0.9474	1.87	0.9693	2.17	0.98500
1.33	0.9082	1.63	0.9484	1.88	0.9699	2.18	0.98537
1.34	0.9099	1.64	0.9495	1.89	0.9706	2.19	0.98574
1.35	0.9115	1.65	0.9505	1.90	0.9713	2.20	0.98610
1.36	0.9131	1.66	0.9515	1.91	0.9719	2.21	0.98645
1.37	0.9147	1.67	0.9525	1.92	0.9726	2.22	0.98679
1.38	0.9162	1.68	0.9535	1.93	0.9732	2.23	0.98713
1.39	0.9177	1.69	0.9545	1.94	0.9738	2.24	0.98745
1.40	0.9192	1.70	0.9554	1.95	0.9744	2.25	0.98778
1.41	0.9207	1.71	0.9564	1.96	0.9750	2.26	0.98809
1.42	0.9222	1.72	0.9573	1.97	0.9756	2.27	0.98840
1.43	0.9236	1.73	0.9582	1.98	0.9761	2.28	0.98870
1.44	0.9251	1.74	0.9591	1.99	0.9767	2.29	0.98899
1.45	0.9265	1.75	0.9599	2.00	0.97725	2.30	0.98928
1.46	0.9279	1.76	0.9608	2.01	0.97778	2.31	0.98956
1.47	0.9292	1.77	0.9616	2.02	0.97831	2.32	0.98983
1.48	0.9306	1.78	0.9625	2.03	0.97882	2.33	0.99010
1.49	0.9319	1.79	0.9633	2.04	0.97932	2.34	0.99036

Table 1: The Normal Distribution Function / continued …

Z	Area	Z	Area	Z	Area	Z	Area
2.35	0.99061	2.55	0.99461	2.75	0.99702	2.95	0.99841
2.36	0.99086	2.56	0.99477	2.76	0.99711	2.96	0.99846
2.37	0.99111	2.57	0.99492	2.77	0.99720	2.97	0.99851
2.38	0.99134	2.58	0.99506	2.78	0.99728	2.98	0.99856
2.39	0.99158	2.59	0.99520	2.79	0.99736	2.99	0.99861
2.40	0.99180	2.60	0.99534	2.80	0.99744	3.0	0.99865
2.41	0.99202	2.61	0.99547	2.81	0.99752	3.1	0.99903
2.42	0.99224	2.62	0.99560	2.82	0.99760	3.2	0.99931
2.43	0.99245	2.63	0.99573	2.83	0.99767	3.3	0.99952
2.44	0.99266	2.64	0.99585	2.84	0.99774	3.4	0.99966
2.45	0.99286	2.65	0.99598	2.85	0.99781	3.5	0.99977
2.46	0.99305	2.66	0.99609	2.86	0.99788	3.6	0.99984
2.47	0.99324	2.67	0.99621	2.87	0.99795	3.7	0.99989
2.48	0.99343	2.68	0.99632	2.88	0.99801	3.8	0.99993
2.49	0.99361	2.69	0.99643	2.89	0.99807	3.9	0.99995
2.50	0.99379	2.70	0.99653	2.90	0.99813		
2.51	0.99396	2.71	0.99664	2.91	0.99819		
2.52	0.99413	2.72	0.99674	2.92	0.99825		
2.53	0.99430	2.73	0.99683	2.93	0.99831		
2.54	0.99446	2.74	0.99693	2.94	0.99836		

Source: Cambridge Elementary Statistical Tables, Lindley and Miller, Cambridge University Press

Table 2: Percentage Points of the t-Distribution (upper tail values)

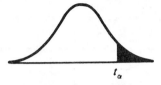

Degrees of Freedom	$t_{0.025}$	$t_{0.005}$
1	12.706	63.657
2	4.303	9.925
3	3.182	5.841
4	2.776	4.604
5	2.571	4.032
6	2.447	3.707
7	2.365	3.499
8	2.306	3.355
9	2.262	3.250
10	2.228	3.169
11	2.201	3.106
12	2.179	3.055
13	2.160	3.012
14	2.145	2.977
15	2.131	2.947
20	2.086	2.845
25	2.060	2.787
30	2.042	2.750
∞	1.960	2.576

Table 3: Percentage Points of the χ^2 Distribution (upper tail values)

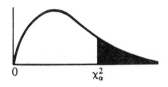

d.f.	.050	.010
1	3.84	6.63
2	5.99	9.21
3	7.81	11.3
4	9.49	13.3
5	11.1	15.1
6	12.6	16.8
7	14.1	18.5
8	15.5	20.1
9	16.9	21.7
10	18.3	23.3
11	19.7	24.7
12	21.0	26.2
13	22.4	27.7
14	23.7	29.1
15	25.0	30.6
16	26.3	32.0
17	27.6	33.4
18	28.9	34.8
19	30.1	36.2
20	31.4	37.6
21	32.7	38.9
22	33.9	40.3
23	35.2	41.6
24	36.4	43.0
25	37.7	44.3
30	43.8	50.9
40	55.8	63.7
50	67.5	76.2
60	79.1	88.4
70	90.5	100
80	102	112
90	113	124
100	124	136

Table 4:   5% Points for the Distribution of F

d f for denom-inator	d f for numerator						
	1	2	3	4	5	6	7
1	161	200	216	225	230	234	237
2	18.51	19.00	19.16	19.25	19.30	19.33	19.36
3	10.13	9.55	9.12	9.01	8.94	8.88	8.84
4	7.71	6.94	6.59	6.26	6.16	6.09	6.04
5	6.61	5.79	5.41	5.19	5.05	4.95	4.88
6	5.99	5.14	4.76	4.53	4.39	4.28	4.21
7	5.59	4.74	4.35	4.12	3.97	3.87	3.79
8	5.32	4.46	4.07	3.84	3.60	3.58	3.50
9	5.12	4.26	3.86	3.63	3.48	3.37	3.29
10	4.96	4.10	3.71	3.48	3.33	3.22	3.14
20	4.35	3.49	3.10	2.87	2.71	2.60	2.52
40	4.08	3.23	2.84	2.61	2.45	2.34	2.25
100	3.94	3.00	2.70	2.46	2.30	2.19	2.10
∞	3.84	2.99	2.37	2.21	2.09	2.01	1.94

Table 4:   5% Points for the Distribution of F / continued ...

d f for denom -inator	d f for numerator						
	8	9	10	20	40	100	∞
1	239	241	242	248	251	253	254
2	19.37	19.38	19.39	19.44	19.47	19.49	19.50
3	8.84	8.81	8.78	8.66	8.60	8.56	8.53
4	6.04	6.00	5.96	5.80	5.71	5.66	5.63
5	4.82	4.78	4.74	4.56	4.46	4.40	4.36
6	4.15	4.10	4.06	3.87	3.77	3.71	3.67
7	3.73	3.68	3.63	3.44	3.34	3.28	3.23
8	3.44	3.39	3.34	3.15	3.05	2.98	2.93
9	3.23	3.18	3.13	2.93	2.82	2.76	2.71
10	3.07	3.02	2.97	2.77	2.67	2.59	2.54
20	2.45	2.40	2.35	2.12	1.99	1.90	1.84
40	2.18	2.12	2.07	1.84	1.69	1.59	1.51
100	2.03	1.97	1.92	1.68	1.51	1.39	1.28
∞	1.94	1.88	1.83	1.57	1.40	1.24	1.00

INDEX